The Feathered
Serpent
and the Cross

The Pre-Columbian God-Kings

The Papal States

The Rise and Fall of Empires

The Feathered Serpent and the Cross

The Pre-Columbian God-Kings

The Papal States

Joyce Milton
The Pre-Columbian God-Kings

Robert A. Orsi
Norman Harrison
The Papal States

Preface by Jeffrey R. Parsons
Professor of Anthropology
The University of Michigan

CASSELL
LONDON

CASSELL LTD.
35 Red Lion Square, London WC1R 4SG
and at Sydney, Auckland, Toronto, Johannesburg,
an affiliate of
Macmillan Publishing Co., Inc.,
New York.

First published in Great Britain 1980

ISBN 0 304 30724 6

Printed in Italy.

Authors: Joyce Milton, Robert A. Orsi, Norman Harrison
Picture Researcher: Janet Adams
Assistant Picture Researcher: Lynn Bowdery

Historical Consultant: Ron William Walden

Design Implementation: Designworks

Rizzoli Editore

Authors of the Italian Edition
    Introduction: Professor Ovidio Dallera
    The Pre-Columbian God-Kings: Dr. Alberto Vacchi,
        Professor Ovidio Dallera
    The Papal States: Dr. Gian Franco Venè
    Maps: Gian Franco Leonardi
Idea and Realization: Harry C. Lindinger
Graphic Design: Gerry Valsecchi
General Editorial Supervisor: Ovidio Dallera

Contents

Preface

Unlike many complex societies of the Old World, the indigenous civilizations of Mexico, Central America, and the Andes region are largely prehistoric. Significant advances have been made in unlocking the dynastic and ritualistic information coded into the carved, modeled, painted, woven, and knotted designs of archaeological findings; we must still, however, rely on the mute remains of stone, brick, pottery, bone, metal, and plants for most of our understanding about how these impressive Amerindian cultural systems evolved during the millenniums prior to European contact in the sixteenth century A.D. Even though a wealth of relevant written information was compiled during the sixteenth and seventeenth centuries, this material can be used only with great caution in reconstructing the earlier past. Few knowledgeable scholars today can agree about what happened in Mesoamerica and the Andes before the Spanish conquest of the New World.

The past two decades have witnessed an almost staggering increase in hard-won knowledge about pre-Columbian America. At the same time, this supplementary information has served to highlight several critical areas where our gaps in understanding are particularly noticeable. Two principal deterrents to the continued investigation of Amerindian civilization remain: (1) an uncritical acceptance—by both the scholarly community and the interested public—of inadequately demonstrated assertions about the pre-Columbian past and (2) the tragic destruction of archaeological sites in the course of modern development. It is apparent that any substantial progress toward eliminating these obstacles can come about only with improved communication between the public and those who seriously study pre-Columbian civilization.

Few ancient cultures anywhere in the world have aroused more interest than those of the Mayas, Aztecs, and Incas—and fewer still have been so intellectually abused under the guise of systematic study. Precisely because the pre-Columbian civilizations are so imprecisely documented, they have provided fertile ground for imaginative investigators to find whatever they are looking for. Even enlightened scholars have resorted to European- or Asiatic-biased models to reconstruct ancient American cultures. It

had been—and still remains—difficult for Western researchers to comprehend Amerindian civilization in its own terms.

During the past twenty years, the study of pre-Columbian America has been brought into the mainstream of international social science. It has been argued, and sometimes convincingly demonstrated, that the specifics of ancient American culture can be interpreted in the light of universal principles. Generalizations and hypotheses of broad applicability over time and space have been formulated, tested, refined, and elaborated on the basis of pre-Columbian Mesoamerican and Andean data. Reports of archaeological and ethnohistorical investigations of Mayan, Aztec, and Incan societies are now read by sociologists, demographers, geographers, economists, and political scientists, as well as by historians and anthropologists. Conversely, archaeologists interested in pre-Columbian civilization now find themselves reading the works of other social scientists.

A generation ago, our knowledge of the Mayas, Aztecs, and Incas was based largely on a handful of ethnohistorical documents, scattered examples of monumental architecture, and a restricted range of ceramic and stone artifacts. A disproportionate number of material remains were known from isolated contexts and had limited import beyond their aesthetic and antiquarian value or their usefulness as indicators of relative chronology. No clearly defined view of pre-Columbian sociopolitical organization and daily life existed. Today we can see more readily that the Mayas, Aztecs, and Incas of the sixteenth century were the products of several millenniums of indigenous Amerindian cultural development that began with the advent of sedentary agricultural life in the fourth millennium B.C. and terminated with the arrival of the Spaniards.

There is nothing about the social organization of pre-Columbian American peoples that is not amenable to understanding in terms of culturological theory. These societies are neither more nor less than examples of preindustrial states, set in particular localities and shaped and molded over time by adaptations to the continuities and changes of natural and cultural environments. Pre-Columbian achievements in architecture, crafts, and the arts have been appreciated by generations of interested people the world over. The last two decades of the twentieth century should provide a much more complete sense of how these impressive artifacts fit into the broad context of Mayan, Aztec, and Incan culture.

JEFFREY R. PARSONS
Professor of Anthropology
The University of Michigan

The Pre-Columbian God-Kings

"They ... came swimming out to the boats of our fleet and brought us parrots, balls of cotton yarn, spears, and many other things, which we exchanged for others that we gave them." So reads the entry in the logbook of Christopher Columbus for Friday, October 12, 1492, the day of the first recorded contact between Europeans and the inhabitants of the New World. "I did not find any bestial men among them, as some of us had expected," the admiral added, "but on the contrary great deference and kindness."

Columbus' descriptions of the primitive but well-favored natives at first convinced many Europeans

that a race of noble savages had been discovered—inhabitants of a "golden world" free of the burden of original sin. By the second decade of the sixteenth century, however, as Spanish colonists began to strike out beyond their settlements in the West Indies, it became obvious that this characterization or any similar labeling was inadequate. Mesoamerica—Mexico and northern Central America—proved to be the home of a confusing variety of peoples, each with its own history and customs and all tied together by a network of economic and military relationships as complex as anything known in Europe.

The most tantalizing reports obtained by the first Spanish explorers concerned rich and powerful New World empires. As early as 1511, two years before his successful traverse of the Isthmus of Panama, Vasco Nuñez de Balboa was told by a local chieftain of a legendary kingdom in the south where "the people eat and drink out of golden vessels and where gold is as cheap as iron is with you." Seven years later, Juan de Grijalva, sailing along the coast of Veracruz and Tabasco in eastern Mexico, heard tales of a fabulously wealthy imperial city that lay somewhere in central Mexico.

As word of the New World's civilizations and supposed riches was brought back to Europe, numerous

Preceding page, Amerind natives laboring for the Spanish conquerors, as depicted in Fray Diego Durán's History of the Indies of New Spain *(1581).*

Popocatépetl (above left), "the smoking mountain," became active on the eve of the Spanish landfall, arousing fears of the god Quetzalcoatl's return. Above, a landscape in the Sierra Madre, the major mountain system of Mexico. Left, a scene in eastern Mexico.

Right, a canyon in the eastern part of the Sierra Madre. Top right, a Pacific lagoon in the Mexican state of Guerrero.

arcane theories were proposed to account for the origin of the natives. A Franciscan friar named Diego Durán, who suggested that the Aztecs were descendants of a lost tribe of Israel, traveled through Mexico in search of a copy of the Hebrew scriptures to document his belief. No such evidence was ever found, but this did not discourage others from speculations of their own. More recently, it has been proposed that the civilizations of the New World owed their existence to contacts with exiles from the lost kingdom of Atlantis, the "Continent of Mu," or visitors from outer space. Some have attempted to link the rise of pre-Columbian kingdoms to the influence of migra-

tions from China, Africa, or Polynesia.

Although the appeal of such theories remains undiminished in the popular mind, serious students agree that civilization in the Western Hemisphere was created independently by the descendants of hunter-gatherers who crossed into the New World from Siberia some time after the close of the last ice age. These migrants dispersed throughout the hemisphere, with two major centers of intensive agricultural development eventually emerging: one in the Andean regions of South America and one in Mesoamerica. Dates for the appearance of the first cultivated plants in these regions are still disputed, but radiocarbon evidence shows that corn, a native Mexican plant that evolved into a staple food crop, was grown in Mesoamerica by 3000 B.C. By that time, settlements on the coast of Peru were already raising

some varieties of beans and gourds; by 1500 B.C., corn too was cultivated. From these humble beginnings eventually arose the three great pre-Columbian "empires"—Mayan, Aztec, and Incan—whose existence was to dazzle and perplex the Spaniards of the sixteenth century.

The Mayas first met the Europeans face to face in 1511, after survivors from a Spanish shipwreck were washed ashore on the Yucatán Peninsula. When a small band of soldier-explorers led by Francisco Fernández de Córdoba made its way along the same coast in 1517, the Mayas lured the Spaniards into their villages and attacked them with spears, arrows, and obsidian-bladed wooden swords.

The fate of the Córdoba mission was only a foretaste of the difficulties the Spaniards were about to

encounter. Although the height of their civilization and power was long in the past, the Mayas proved to be the most stubborn and formidable obstacle in the path of Spanish conquest. In 1526, Francisco de Montejo launched a campaign to subjugate the natives of the Yucatán Peninsula, only to retreat after nine years of frustrating and inconclusive jungle warfare. A second expedition, launched by Montejo's son, succeeded only because the Mayas failed to put aside their internal feuds to mount a concerted defense. The younger Montejo routinely ordered Mayan chieftains burned alive and had his men cut off the arms and legs of Mayan soldiers. After horrific slaughter, the northern Yucatán was finally subdued, but pockets of resistance still remained in the interior. One tribe, the Itzás, retreated to Lake Petén in present-day Guatemala, where they resisted conquest

Palenque, an ancient Mayan city in the rain forest of Chiapas State in Mexico, flourished during the later part of the Classic Period (ca. A.D. 300–900). Its stone reliefs (far left, above and below) and stucco carvings are among the finest achievements of Mayan artists. The Temple of Inscriptions (center) stands over the underground crypt of a great chief. This page, top, a view into the plaza of the temple's northwest wing. Immediately above, the Temple of the Sun, with the remains of an elaborately sculpted stucco wall known as a roof comb.

until 1697. In some places, sporadic rebellions persisted into the twentieth century.

The ancestors of this proud people once occupied a vast territory of about 120,000 square miles, stretching from the Pacific coast of Guatemala and El Salvador through the lowlands of the Petén region to the flat, arid limestone shelf of the Yucatán Peninsula.

13

Preceding pages, a gallery of Mayan faces modeled in stone, ceramic, stucco, and jade. Above, a statuette, perhaps Mayan in origin. Uxmal, site of the Temple of the Magician (left) and the Nunnery Quadrangle (below), epitomizes the refinement of late Classic architecture in the Yucatán. Below left, a detail of a corbeled arch and a geometric frieze.

Mayan lands included parts of Honduras and all of Belize and reached northward into the Mexican states of Chiapas and Tabasco. Much of this territory, especially the Petén lowlands, which were to become the heartland of Classic Mayan civilization, is so unproductive and inhospitable that the climb to civilization can only have been accomplished through unremitting struggle.

The first settlers, perhaps emigrants from the highlands, arrived in the Río Pasíon valley of Guatemala in about 1000 B.C. For nearly five hundred years, the lowland settlements were little more than isolated frontier villages whose inhabitants lived in roughly egalitarian tribal groups. Then, in about 550 B.C., something caused a dramatic change in the lowlands way of life.

One plausible hypothesis suggests that the Mayas in the lowlands experienced a population explosion that profoundly altered their relationship to the environment. According to this theory, population pressures led to a severe shortage of fresh water, and it became necessary for the Mayas to band together to maintain existing water holes and to build artificial reservoirs. The need for large-scale work projects, combined with increasing competition for scarce resources, touched off a political and social revolution. Power came to be concentrated in the hands of an elite class that adopted a lifestyle, a religious outlook, and forms of government suitable to its new status.

Whatever its precise causes, this transformation, once begun, was accomplished very quickly. By A.D. 300—and in some areas as early as A.D. 100—the Mayas' sculpture, pottery, writing system, and architecture had been revolutionized. The most notable development, however, was the appearance of architectural complexes consisting of monumental limestone buildings with stucco façades and corbeled roofs. In addition to these rectangular, multiroomed structures, the complexes contained tall temple-pyramids with ornate stucco walls known as roof combs; steles, or stone slab markers, bearing finely carved hieroglyphic inscriptions; broad ceremonial plazas; and, often, elevated causeways connecting the major structures.

Although the Spanish conquistadors never saw these complexes in use, they recognized in them the work of a highly organized and advanced society. "If Yucatán were to gain a name and reputation from the multitude, the grandeur and the beauty of its buildings," wrote the Franciscan brother Diego de Landa in 1566, " . . . its glory would spread like that of Peru and New Spain." Subsequent exploration proved that Landa had seen only a small part of the Mayan accomplishment.

Mayan architecture of the Classic Period (ca. A.D. 300–900) is characterized by a variety of styles. For example, the so-called Puuc-style structures of the Yucatán, which Landa had seen, are notable for their formal organization and decorations and for their large, relatively spacious interior rooms. Copán in Honduras has ornately carved steles and altars but contains few structures even remotely suitable for habitation. Uaxactún, near the northern border of Guatemala, is the site of a massive labyrinthine complex that has been compared to the Mycenaean "great houses" of Bronze Age Europe. The Río Béc area, which lies between the Mexican states of Campeche and Quintana Roo in south-central Yucatán, has numerous tall-towered edifices—some with stairways too steep to climb—surmounted with dummy "temples." Still another style of building is represented by Tikal, a sprawling complex of five tall temple-pyramids and three thousand lesser structures that lies in the Petén region of Guatemala. Tikal, which was not even seen by Europeans until the late seventeenth century and has only recently been excavated, is now recognized as the epitome of the Greater Petén style, the most widespread style of the Classic Period.

There has been a good deal of animated debate about the function of Mayan architecture. Until recently, the most persuasive scholars maintained that the so-called Mayan palaces could never have been inhabited. They contended that the Mayas lived in perishable structures of wood and adobe, reserving their stone edifices for religious, ceremonial, and civic purposes. Lately, though, many archaeologists have come to believe that past emphasis on the Mayas' mystical and religious beliefs fostered a rather myopic view of Mayan civilization. Most likely, the Mayan sites can be identified with ancient city-states, and Mayan palaces served as the residences of an elite group of ruling families and their functionaries.

This ruling class lived well, even luxuriously, but did not require elaborate furnishings or indoor kitchen facilities. Cooking, and perhaps sanitary functions, may have been relegated to wooden shacks that stood apart from the main buildings. Low stone benches or platforms were the only major pieces of furniture, suggesting that it was customary to sit cross-legged and to sleep at night on thin cotton mats of quilted cushions. Mayan chieftains and their families no doubt spent much of their time outdoors, and there is some evidence that the palace courtyards were originally shaded by cloth awnings.

The Mayan elite comprised working rulers who devoted themselves to organizing the civil and religious affairs of their subjects, perhaps with the assis-

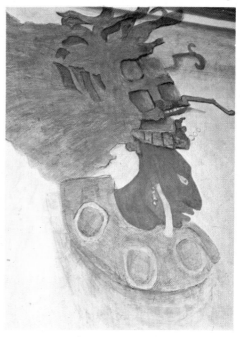

The success of a Mayan war party of 1,100 years ago is vividly depicted in these mural paintings from Bonampak, a minor site in Chiapas not discovered until 1946. Near left, a war raid. Below, white-robed aristocrats preparing to offer sacrifice. The festive dress of a war captain (above) includes a cloak with shell medallions. Above far left, a participant in the victory ceremonies, with a hoop of quetzal feathers strapped to his back. Below far left, another Mayan figure, possibly a dancer.

Mayan ceremonies and sacrifices

The first Spanish priests in the Yucatán were amazed, to discover that the Mayas practiced some rites that seemed to parallel those of Christianity. There was a form of confession, for example, made by an individual once during his lifetime, usually on his deathbed. In essence, though, Mayan religion was not a private matter but a public one. Virtually every aspect of human activity was bound up with ceremonies, fasts, and feast days.

The most solemn rituals involved human sacrifice. A more common ceremony was the ritual dance, in which scores of dancers dressed in grotesque masks often participated. Although the rules governing all ceremonies were strict, these dances nonetheless appear to have been a source of entertainment. *On the Things of Yucatán,* written about 1566 by Bishop Diego de Landa, notes that many of the performers were accomplished mimics and that some introduced witty asides on the proceedings.

Above left, a god perched atop a ceramic burial urn. The vessel's sides are decorated with rows of human skulls and a leering jaguar's head—a reference to the sun's nightly journey through the underworld. Left, a small altar from Tonina, Chiapas. Above, a ruler named Shield Jaguar receiving a ceremonial offering.

Right, a Mayan woman holding a jaguar head. This stone relief from Yaxchilán illustrates the artificially flattened forehead that the Mayas considered the height of beauty. Although naturally brachycephalic, the Mayas achieved this effect by binding the heads of their infants between boards.

tance of a class of "civil servants." Some of the palace rooms were used for audience halls, others for storing elaborate ceremonial costumes and other luxury goods. The broad outdoor plazas may have been used as outdoor markets, where the great majority of people, who lived in clusters of outlying hamlets, thronged to exchange goods and conversation.

Many Mayan cities appear to have had facilities for the leisure activities of the upper class. Some sites have sweat baths, and at least one contains a room probably used as an indoor shower house. Almost every major city had its ball court, where two teams would compete in a game whose object was to propel a hard rubber ball through a stone hoop mounted high on the court wall. This game, which had many variations throughout Mesoamerica, probably served religious as well as sporting functions. According to some accounts, the spectators enjoyed wagering on the outcome. For participants, the stakes were high: Losing players might have their hands—or even their heads—cut off.

Religion played a central role in the lives of the ancient Mayas. Members of the priesthood married and enjoyed a luxurious lifestyle, but they were called upon to undergo rigorous periods of preparation for their ceremonial roles. Mayan priests holed up inside the dark, musty chambers atop the temple-pyramids long in advance of a major festival day, purifying themselves by fasting, abstaining from sexual intercourse, and performing acts of self-mutilation. Thus prepared, they would carry out their solemn rituals: elaborate dancing; testing rites, such as walking barefoot over a bed of hot coals; and acts of sympathetic magic to influence the gods. To assure ade-

Left, a temple at Xlapac in Yucatán State ornamented by masks of the rain god. Above, a warrior and his captive. The richly carved stone reliefs of Yaxchilán record the exploits of the powerful Jaguar dynasty, which flourished during the eighth century A.D.

quate rainfall, for example, functionaries called *chacs* would empty gourds of water over a fire, thereby acting out the belief that Chac, the rain god, watered the earth by sprinkling it with rain from the celestial gourd he carried.

The most important Mayan ceremonies involved human sacrifices, for it was believed that the gods must periodically be nourished by human blood. However, in contrast to Aztec gods, whose demand for the "precious fluid" was insatiable, Mayan deities were usually satisfied with the sacrifice of a few prisoners of war, slaves, or children.

Mayan priests were also the guardians of learning, charged with computing the days of the calendar, carrying out rites of divination, and ensuring that activities were properly recorded. A large percentage of the Mayan writings that have so far been deci-

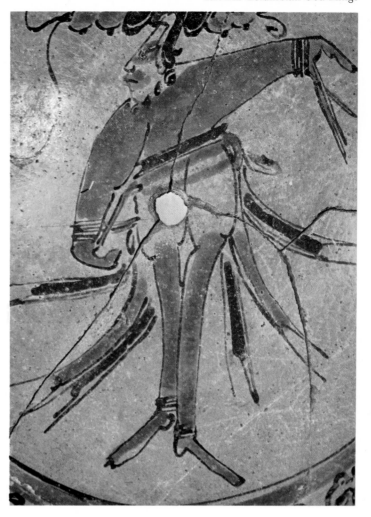

This painted figure (above) is from a terracotta plate found at Uaxactún in Guatemala. This ceremonial vessel was ritually "killed" by boring a hole through the center of the figure.

Above, a five-story temple at Edzna in the western Yucatán, as it appeared before restoration. Right, a handcoiled polychrome vase.

Toltec exiles led by Kukulcan introduced to the Yucatán a culture even more militaristic than that of the native Maya. A fusion of Toltec and Mayan styles occurred at Chichén-Itzá, where the Temple of the Warriors (right) recalls the grand monuments at the Toltec capital of Tula. Details of bas-reliefs from Chichén-Itzá show a warrior carrying an enemy's head (center left) and a serpent-bird with a human figure (center right). Bottom, a Chac Mool, or recumbent Toltec figure, holding a bowl.

phered deals with astronomical observations and calendrical calculations—often recording dates that long precede the rise of Mayan civilization. Early studies of the Mayan system of writing suggested that the literate class was wholly caught up in the pursuit of such esoteric studies and did not even consider secular events worth recording. This interpretation, which did so much to foster the image of the "mysterious Mayas," has proved unjustified. Since the late 1950s, scholars have discovered that many of the steles do indeed record the dates of the births, deaths, and accessions of important rulers. The work of reconstructing Mayan history has just begun, but someday we may hope to have a fairly complete record of the names and exploits of individual Mayan rulers.

Another discovery that has led to a revised interpretation of Mayan history was made by the Mexican archaeologist Alberto Ruz in 1952. Excavating at the Temple of Inscriptions at Palenque, a site in the state of Chiapas in southeastern Mexico, Ruz found a rubble-filled hidden staircase leading downward from the inner chamber of the temple. After four field seasons of patient labor, Ruz entered the cleared stairway and followed it to a subterranean burial vault. In the passage leading to the vault he discovered the bones of five human beings, perhaps attendants stationed there to guard the vault from evil spirits. The crypt itself housed a stone sarcophagus, which Ruz opened to reveal the remains of a great king, dressed for eternity in a treasure of jade, including a fine burial mask, ornamental ear spools, a mouth stopper, and many necklaces. A jade figure of a sun god lay at the dead man's side.

Ruz's discovery raised the possibility that the Mayas' temple-pyramids were funerary monuments, serving much the same function as the pyramids of Egypt. Other temple burials have since been found, and no doubt many more exist—although the problems connected with excavating the tombs without destroying the pyramids can be formidable. Interestingly, some of the temples at Palenque have been found to contain psychoducts, small tubes reaching

Right, the Castillo at Chichén-Itzá. The Red Jaguar Throne (detail above), made of painted limestone, was discovered inside this temple during archaeological work in 1936. The jaguar's spots are indicated by disks of apple green jade.

Astronomy and the Mayan calendar

In the Mayan world view, time was a kind of cosmic relay race run ceaselessly by teams of gods. The belief that events were determined by the gods associated with given dates made keeping track of this relay race a matter of the greatest importance.

There were two distinct systems for measuring the year: The astronomical year consisted of 365 days, and the "almanac" year comprised 260 days. The astronomical and almanac years coincided only once every 18,980 days (every fifty-two astronomical years)—an occurrence that was fraught with anxiety. To measure longer periods of time, the Mayas used a calendar based on a cycle of thirteen *baktuns,* or 144,000-day periods. According to archaeologist Eric Thompson, the present Great Cycle of 5,200 astronomical years, thought to coincide with the life of the present universe, began in 3113 B.C. and will end in A.D. 2011.

The Caracol (above) at Chichén-Itzá was used as an observatory. Its name, meaning "snail," refers to the interior spiral staircase that leads to a series of observation windows. The archaeologist Eric Thompson described this disagreeable blend of Puuc-Maya and early Toltec styles as "a two-decker wedding cake on the square carton in which it came."

Facing page, above, two elaborately dressed personages conferring over an altar piled with human thigh bones and a skull. This relief, about five and a half feet in diameter, is from Altar #5 at Tikal. Left, a stone with four glyphs.

Near left and center left, examples of Mayan glyph writing on limestone.

Copán in Honduras is noted for its sculpture and carved glyphs (center, above and below). The Stair of Hieroglyphics (above) is carved with at least two thousand hieroglyphic characters. This relief from Palenque (facing page) shows a Mayan figure with heavy ear pendants.

from the burial vaults to just below the floor of the temple chambers. Such tubes may have been used for communicating with the spirits of the dead.

The body that Ruz found at Palenque was that of a ruler who died during the late seventh or early eighth century A.D. This ruler could be described as a king or a great chief, but he was not an emperor, for the Mayan domains formed an empire only in the cultural sense. At their height, the Mayan cities were never under centralized rule. Relations among the elites of the various city-states seem to have been quite competitive.

At the base of Mayan society, separated by an ever-widening gulf from their rulers, were the commoners, known as the *yalca uinicob,* or lower men. Their lives were devoted to agriculture, which was practiced in the form of slash-and-burn cultivation. It is usually assumed that the staple crop was corn, a grain so important that it was worshiped as a god. Another possibility, however, is that the Mayas consumed large quantities of ramon nuts, a high-protein fruit that grows on the indigenous ramon tree. If so, the corn diet may have been a prerogative of the elite class, and the daily existence of the average farmer was not so closely tied to the arduous labor of burning out jungle clearings and protecting cultivated plots from grazing deer. The ramon nut hypothesis helps explain how the jungles could have supported a population large and leisured enough to spare the labor needed for constructing so many monumental works.

The Mayas did not comport themselves as lords of creation but as an integral part of a larger cosmic

plan. Important activities like corn-planting were strictly limited to auspicious days, and the Mayan hunter was careful to ask forgiveness of the animals that he killed. It was this emphasis on moderation and self-control that encouraged generations of writers to describe the Mayas as a democratic, aesthetically inclined, and pacifistic people—the "Greeks of the Americas." The evidence, however, presents quite a different picture.

Dramatic proof of the importance of warfare in the late Classic Period has been found at Bonampak, an otherwise minor ceremonial site located in Chiapas State. A series of splendid murals there narrates the story of a battle, beginning with a group of warriors marching forth and ending with an elaborate victory celebration. These last scenes show a great chief dressed in a jaguar-skin jacket and wearing a hoop of sacred quetzal feathers strapped to his back. Around him are ranged well-dressed noblemen, dancers in fancy ceremonial headdresses, and the raid's booty—human captives. One prisoner has already been decapitated, another appears to be pleading desperately for his life, and several more have had their fingernails torn out and are staring in horror at their bleeding hands.

It is difficult to judge how common such scenes

Rising above the dense jungle of Guatemala's Petén region, Tikal's Temple I (right) stands 170 feet tall. Unlike the many monuments at Tikal that were built in layers over older structures, Temple I was erected all at one time, in about A.D. 700. In 1962, excavators from the University of Pennsylvania discovered a splendid tomb hidden beneath this temple. Below, a funerary urn.

were in real life. The Mayas of the Classic Period apparently did not possess standing armies, and it is likely that their wars consisted mostly of sporadic raids organized to secure captives. Casualties in the heat of battle were probably few.

The Mayan city-states were by no means isolated from their neighbors. Avid traders, the Mayas engaged in commerce both among themselves and with various Mesoamerican cities, including Teotihuacán in central Mexico. Important trade goods included salt from the Yucatán, jade, cotton clothing, slaves, and honey from the Yucatán's stingless bees.

Cacao beans served both as a major trade item and as a form of currency among the Mayas. Cocoa was a much-coveted beverage throughout Mesoamerica, but presumably only the wealthy could afford to drink it with any regularity. The less well-off used the beans as a handy means of exchange. There is scattered evidence that the "chocolate standard" was sometimes debased by counterfeiters, who carefully removed the skins of cacao beans and glued them over false cores of wax or avocado rind.

Throughout the seventh and eighth centuries, the ceremonial centers of the central lowlands bustled with activity. Then, during the ninth century, the

Above left, one of Tikal's many limestone steles. Left, a detail of the stele, which stands on Tikal's Great Plaza, near the North Acropolis (above). Right, a view into the unroofed enclosure of a twin-pyramid complex at Tikal. A stele and an altar can be seen through the doorway.

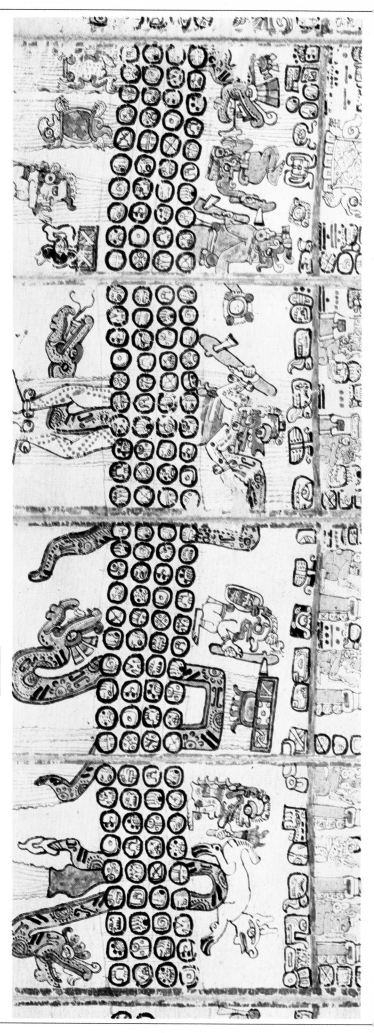

Fantastic serpents and figures (details above and below) illustrate these pages from the Madrid Codex (right). This late Mayan manuscript (ca. A.D. 1400) treats divination rituals connected with hunting, beekeeping, weaving, rainmaking, crops, and diseases. It is painted on paper made from pounded tree bark and contains fifty-six pages decorated on both sides and folded like an accordian. Fully extended, the manuscript is about twenty-three feet long.

The Mayan codices

"We found large numbers of books . . . and they contained nothing in which there was not to be seen superstition and lies of the devil, so we burned them all . . . ." Thus wrote Bishop Diego de Landa, who had personally signed the order for the destruction of Mayan codices in 1562. Landa was zealous in his efforts to destroy written works having to do with the traditional Mayan religion: Only three Mayan manuscripts exist today.

In his work as a historian, Landa partially compensated for the loss of these precious documents. (The bishop even attempted to preserve a key to Mayan writing.) Ironically, Landa's invaluable work on the history and customs of the Yucatán was completed while he was incarcerated in Spain, awaiting a hearing on charges that he had overstepped his authority in his fervent attacks on paganism.

The Mayas possessed the best-developed writing system in Mesoamerica. Above, four glyphs.

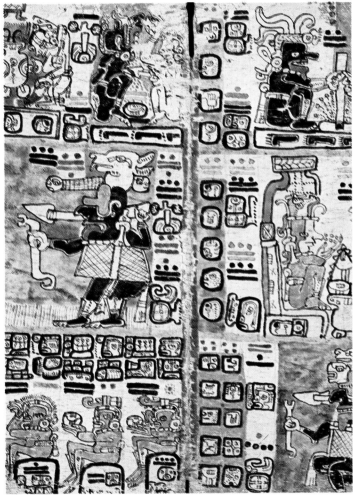

Above, a page from the Madrid Codex. The partially deciphered writings deal primarily with the rotations of Venus and the planet's influence on human affairs. Left, a detail from another segment of the codex. Right, a terra-cotta figure from the island necropolis of Jaina in Campeche State.

sites were abandoned, one by one. Building activity ceased, no new steles were constructed, and the jungle reclaimed the broad plazas and courtyards. Why the centers of the lowlands were forsaken is a mystery. Any number of explanations have been suggested: climatic changes, the exhaustion of fields near the cities, invasion by foreigners from Mexico, and even a social revolution sparked by the burden of forced labor on the temple. As was probably the case a millennium before, a population explosion was likely the deciding factor.

Although the decline of the city-states of the central region remains an enigma, there are some clues to the fate of their sister states in the Yucatán. Here, building activity continued somewhat longer, with foreign influences gradually becoming more evident in the style of the region. In about A.D. 987, the ceremonial center of Chichén-Itzá (then known as Uucil-Abnal) was attacked by an army from the west. These invaders, the Toltecs, were led by a man who called himself Kukulcan—the Mayan word for "feathered serpent," which in the Toltec language is rendered "Quetzalcoatl."

The name of Quetzalcoatl dominates the history of the Toltecs, a Nahua-speaking people that had established its capital at Tula, north of present-day Mexico City, by A.D. 900. The Toltecs were cosmopolitan, accomplished artists and energetic innovators who took many elements from the cultures of their neighbors. The Toltecs' penchant for adopting new gods seems to have caused a deep rift in their society. At the root of the trouble was the cult of Tezcatlipoca, whose name means "Smoking Mirror." This deity was the rival of Quetzalcoatl, the civilizing god, and his cult demanded human sacrifice, a practice opposed by Quetzalcoatl. In the late tenth century, Topiltzin, the ninth king of the Toltecs, adopted the name of Quetzalcoatl and attempted to discourage the new warrior cults. Eventually, however, Topiltzin was driven from Tula by a series of revolts and natural disasters. After the vanquished king departed for the east, a legend arose that Quetzalcoatl would

Many Mayan centers had courts for playing a distinctive type of ball game that was widespread throughout Mesoamerica. This fine eighth-century court (left) is from Copán; the stone hoop (below) is from Chichén-Itzá. Although the game was always played with a hard rubber ball, the rules often varied. In an Aztec version, players were not permitted to touch the ball with their hands. The specific features of the Mayan game are unknown, but this court marker (right) suggests a religious as well as a sporting aspect. Bottom, a player wearing protective padding.

someday return to central Mexico to overthrow his rivals and inaugurate an era when the gods would no longer demand human blood, accepting sacrifices of flowers in its place.

A few years after Topiltzin's departure from Tula, Toltec armies led by Kukulcan appeared in the Yucatán, eight hundred miles away. It cannot be ascertained whether these two Quetzalcoatls were the same individual, but it is known that from this time on the Mayas of the Yucatán were ruled by a Mexican elite. Later, Chichén-Itzá was settled by the Itzás, who were either Mexicans or Mexicanized Mayas and who also had a leader called Kukulcan. The Itzás were by no means welcomed as a civilizing influence by the Mayas. Whereas the Mayas seem to have more or less accepted the Toltecs, they were shocked by the Itzás' religious practices, which apparently included certain erotic rites. *The Books of Chilam Balam*, a body of Mayan writings compiled after the Spanish conquest, vividly expresses the Mayan view of their new ruler, excoriating the Itzás as "the unrestrained lewd

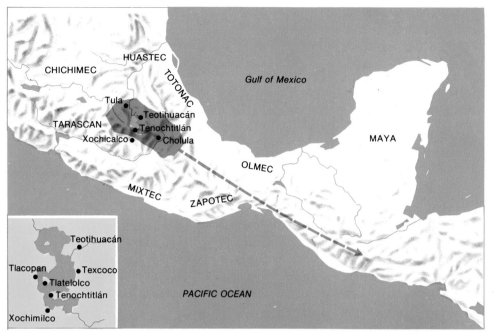

Aztecs

The Tenocha-Aztecs were one of several Nahua-speaking Aztec groups that arrived in the Valley of Mexico during the thirteenth century A.D. In 1368 they founded the city of Tenochtitlán on uninhabited marsh land in Lake Texcoco. By 1519 they had absorbed Tlatelolco, a neighboring city founded by a closely related Aztec group, and were masters of more than fifty formerly independent city-states in the Valley of Mexico (arrow indicates direction of Aztec expansion). Directly or indirectly, the Tenocha-Aztecs also controlled most of central Mexico from the Pacific to the Gulf of Mexico.

Mayas

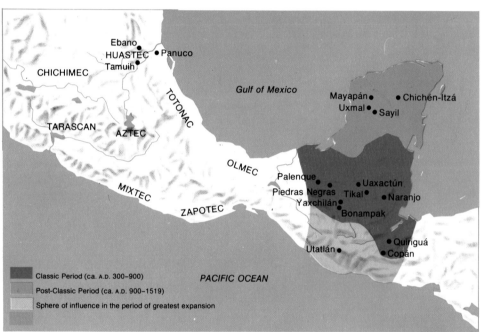

Classic Period (ca. A.D. 300–900)

Post-Classic Period (ca. A.D. 900–1519)

Sphere of influence in the period of greatest expansion

Mayan lands can be divided into three zones: the highlands area of the Pacific coast; the central lowlands of Guatemala and Honduras; and the flat, arid limestone shelf of the Yucatán. The earliest known Mayan sites are in the highlands and date from the second millennium B.C. By 1000 B.C., settlers—probably emigrants from the highlands—had moved into the Río Pasíon region of Guatemala. Mayan civilization of the Classic Period (between approximately A.D. 300 and 900) never achieved political unity. City-states, sometimes allied but frequently at war, were the characteristic units of society.

Mixtecs

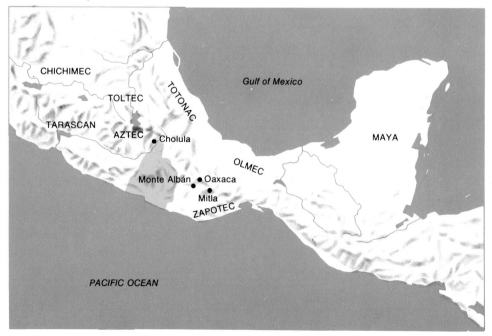

Pushed southward by the expanding empire of the Toltecs, the Mixtecs invaded Zapotec territory and by the eleventh century had created a powerful kingdom of their own. Thanks to eight extant genealogical and historical codices, the history of the Mixtec people is known in some detail. In 1497, for example, the Mixtecs joined forces with a Zapotec king named Cocijoeza to inflict a crushing defeat on the Aztecs. When the Oaxaca region came under Aztec domination, many Mixtec craftsmen were carried off to work at Tenochtitlán.

Olmecs

The Olmecs were the creators of an enduring and highly influential civilization that flourished along the Gulf coast of Mexico in what are now the states of Tabasco and Veracruz. The language the Olmecs spoke is yet unknown and the precise role of this people in Mesoamerican history is still controversial. Apparently, though, the Olmecs were the first in Mesoamerica to develop an elite-class society and to build major urban and ceremonial centers—most notably San Lorenzo, which reached its height between 1200 and 900 B.C., and La Venta, which flourished from 900 to 400 B.C.

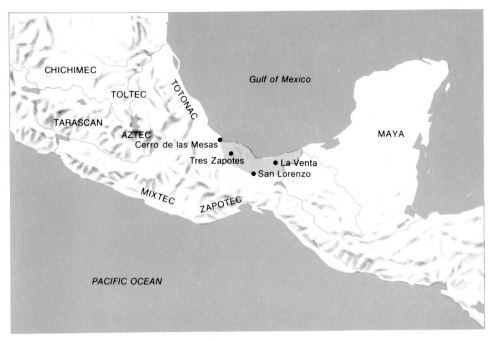

Totonacs

The first major Mesoamerican city to be visited by Cortés and his party on their expedition to the New World in 1519 was Cempoala, a center of the Totonac kingdom known as El Totonacapan. Home to perhaps as many as 100,000 residents, Cempoala was situated on a densely populated flood plain southeast of El Tajín and boasted such advanced features as a highly developed flood-control and irrigation system. By the time of Cortés' arrival, El Totonacapan had become a client state of the Aztec empire and eagerly made common cause with the Spanish invaders.

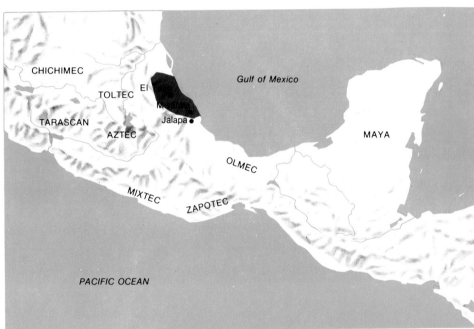

Zapotecs

The Zapotecs were the builders of Monte Albán, a Oaxacan city that rose to power during the third century A.D. and was conquered some time after the beginning of the eighth century. Monte Albán, although never as heavily populated as the great central Mexican city of Teotihuacán, covered an area of some fifteen square miles. The city is noted for its great plazas and underground passageways, as well as its profusion of temples, many built in layers, one atop the other. Despite being conquered by the Mixtecs, the Zapotecs retained their distinct identity as a people.

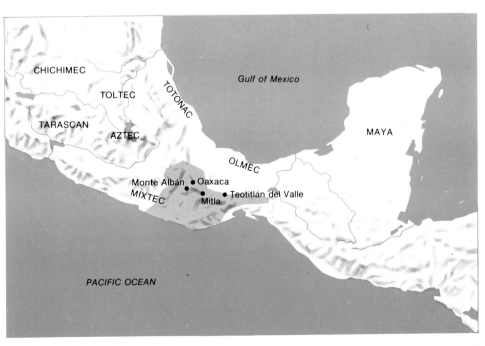

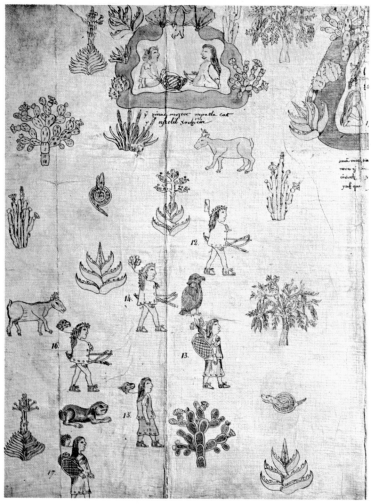

Above left, a drawing from the Mapa Tlotzin relating the establishment of a group of Chichimec rulers in the eastern valley of Mexico. Below left, an unidentified personage wearing a coyote mask. The model, of Toltec workmanship, is made of mother-of-pearl. Below, a painted relief from the ball court of Tula.

ones of the day, the unrestrained lewd ones of the night, the rogues of the world."

The Itzás built the Yucatán's first true city, Mayapán, where more than three thousand dwellings were crowded inside a long defensive wall. Mayapán and Chichén-Itzá were natural rivals. Their antagonism reached its peak during the career of Hunac Ceel, a leader whose rise to power also sheds some light on the rites connected with Chichén-Itzá's celebrated Sacred Well. The well, actually a natural limestone sinkhole, was the site of sacrifices to the rain god in times of drought. Most victims—men, women, and children—were swallowed up by the waters of the sinkhole; those who managed to survive several hours in the well were thought to have become privy to a prophecy from the rain god himself. Hunac Ceel gambled his life on this chance. Volunteering as a sacrifice, he not only stayed alive but emerged from the well with a "prophecy" that led to his acclamation as ruler of Mayapán. In due time, this clever and unscrupulous leader eliminated the lord of Chichén-

Itzá and became the supreme lord of the Yucatán.

The Itzás of Mayapán governed the peninsula for more than two hundred years. Their rule accelerated the decline of Mayan culture. Mayapán's buildings were shoddily constructed, and the artifacts produced in the city were as numerous as they were undistinguished. The city's inhabitants did not engage in farming, living instead on tribute offerings exacted from the subject peoples of the Yucatán. Under this regime the Mayas neglected their native arts, and the activity of the priest-astronomers all but ceased.

The one thing the Mayas did not forget during this period was how to fight. Mayapán was destroyed by a revolt in 1441, and the Yucatán came under the control of sixteen powerful families who constantly feuded among themselves. It was this group of warlike and self-sufficient Mayas who harried Francisco Fernández de Córdoba's expedition in 1517.

According to legend, the Aztecs left their homeland of Aztlán in western Mexico in approximately A.D.

This massive basalt head (left) probably represents a ruler. Monolithic heads of this type, found in the states of Veracruz and Tabasco, are the work of the Olmecs, a people of mysterious origins who flourished at the turn of the first millennium B.C. Above, an anthropomorphic baby jaguar image in serpentine. Below, a twenty-two-inch-tall sculpture depicting the presentation of a "jaguar-baby."

1168 and eventually made their way to central Mexico, a region in ferment, with numerous small city-states vying for living space. Numbering no more than a few thousand individuals at most, the Aztecs could not have been a potent political force. They did have a god, however, who imbued them with a sense of destiny: Huitzilopochtli, or "Hummingbird-on-the-Left." The Aztecs had discovered Huitzilo-pochtli—or more likely an idol representing him—in a cave during their wanderings through central Mexico. In return for a diet of "human hearts . . . freshly sacrificed," the deity promised them a new homeland under his protection.

The Aztecs kept up their part of the bargain with Huitzilopochtli even though this sparked conflict with their more powerful neighbors. By 1349 the re-

Tenacious fighters and respected craftsmen, the Mixtecs were a force to reckon with in Mexico for more than five centuries, dominating the region of Oaxaca until their conquest by the Aztecs. Below, a Mixtec vase. This turquoise and jade inlaid mask (right), thought to represent Quetzalcoatl, is of Aztec workmanship but makes use of techniques developed by the Mixtecs.

taliatory wars touched off by Aztec raiding parties had reduced the Aztecs to desperate straits. Some Aztecs who survived these wars attached themselves as mercenaries to the more powerful Culhuas. After a battle in which Aztec warriors served with particular distinction, the Aztecs petitioned the Culhuac chief, Coxcox, to grant them one of his daughters so that they could found a dynasty. Coxcox agreed, and on the day appointed for the ceremony he arrived in the Aztec camp anticipating a wedding party. As the festivities got under way, the proud father awaited the appearance of the bride. Instead, he was horrified to see a priest, dressed in the girl's flayed skin, dancing the role of the nature goddess, Toci. The Aztecs had meant the gesture as a compliment, but Coxcox was not pleased. He ordered an immediate attack, and his vassals just managed to escape to a swampy island in the center of Lake Texcoco. This event, which took place in the year 1369, marked the founding of Tenochtitlán, the future capital of the Aztec Empire.

Although the marshy islands of Lake Texcoco could not have been a promising site for permanent habitation, the Aztecs saw there an eagle perched atop a prickly-pear cactus—the very sign Huitzilopochtli had told them to look for. This encouraged them to settle down and begin refashioning their environment into the beginnings of a true city. There was little wood or stone to work with, and at first not even enough dry ground could be found to build on. The Aztecs therefore drove piles into the muddy lake bottom and used earth as landfill. More new land was created in the form of *chinampas,* or "floating is-

Above, a turquoise-inlaid pectoral ornament in the form of a double-headed serpent. Coiled rattlesnakes (below) appear frequently in Aztec art.

Aztec artists

"I carve jade, gold I cast in the crucible, I set emeralds ... and this is my song!" These lines in celebration of the creative impulse suggest the respected place occupied by artists in Aztec society. Their very name, *tolteca,* linked the artists with the golden tradition of Toltec culture.

Those who worked with metal, gems, and feathers enjoyed many privileges, including exemption from agricultural labor. The Aztecs did not, however, believe in art for art's sake: The tolteca were valued because their work served the gods.

Center, a stone dog or coyote, a symbol of the warrior order of the Jaguar Knights. Near left, a calcite cacao vase, shaped in part like a rabbit, from the Mexican Gulf coast. According to legend, the rabbit was a sign of fertility.

Immediately below, a pottery ocarina in the shape of a turtle. Bottom, a grasshopper from Chapultepec.

lands"—artificial islets built up from layers of reed mats and mud. A more serious problem was the lack of a fresh-water source and land suitable for growing corn. Since the Lake Texcoco region was dominated by a number of more-powerful city-states, the Aztecs of Tenochtitlán—the Tenochas—were dependent on the good will of their neighbors.

The Tenochas were not alone on Lake Texcoco. On an island just to the north of their new settlement lay Tlatelolco, the home of another group of Aztecs. At first, both Tenochtitlán and Tlatelolco were subject to the Tepanec city-state of Azcapotzalco, whose king, Tezozomoc, nursed imperial ambitions. As a

sign of his regard for the service rendered by Aztec mercenaries, Tezozomoc sent his son to Tlatelolco to reign as the Aztecs' first king. Tezozomoc had meant for his son to have dominion over both Aztec cities, but the Tenochas wanted their own king. When a Culhuac noblewoman and her son appeared in Tenochtitlán as refugees, the Tenochas seized the opportunity to have a ruler who could offer them the legitimacy they had been seeking for so long.

During the 1420s another notable exile arrived in Tenochtitlán: Nezahualcoyotl, son of the late king of Texcoco. Nezahualcoyotl, whose father had been killed by the Tepanecs, convinced the young warriors

Until its destruction by invaders in the eighth century A.D., Teotihuacán (left) was the center of the most influential civilization in central Mexico. The Aztecs believed that four worlds had existed before the current universe and that the Pyramid of the Sun (below) was the birthplace of the present creation. They adopted this abandoned site for their religious rituals.

of Tenochtitlán to desert their Tepanec masters and to join with Texcoco and a third city-state, Tacuba, in a triple alliance. This alliance was basically an agreement to fight together against the Tepanecs and to divide the spoils—two shares each for Tenochtitlán and Texcoco to one share for Tacuba. The most outstanding feature of the alliance proved to be its longevity: It held together until the Spanish conquest, thus becoming the outstanding exception to the treacherous pacts between the city-states of that era.

The beginning of the so-called Tepanec Wars coincided with the transfer of power in Tenochtitlán to a new generation of brash and self-confident aristocrats. One of their number, Itzcoatl, became king in 1427, and another was later to reign as Montezuma I. The most influential, however, was Tlacaelel, Itzcoatl's nephew, a warrior-priest who preferred to remain the power behind the throne. It was Tlacaelel who planned the campaign that led to the fall of the Tepanec capital of Azcapotzalco in 1428, an event that upset the established order in the Valley of Mexico. Tlacaelel's war party was able to reward its supporters with new titles and rich private lands taken from its share of the spoils. By 1433, the Tenocha army, still acting as part of the triple alliance, had captured the neighboring city-states of Xochimilco and Cuitlahuac. Even the Tlatelolcans were

Above left, a courtyard in Teotihuacán's Palace of the Jaguar. Feathered serpents (left and above) are a common motif in Teotihuacán's stonework. An early form of Tlaloc, the Aztec rain god, was also worshiped at this site.

now subject to their parvenu cousins. Although the original goals of the alliance had now been realized, Tlacaelel and his followers were not satisfied. With the Tepanecs vanquished, they began to look outside the Valley of Mexico for new enemies to conquer.

The spectacular victory over Azcapotzalco convinced the Tenochas that they were destined to become the heirs of the Toltecs. But as they looked forward to this great destiny, the memories of their ignominious flight to Lake Texcoco and their years of scavenging for food continued to haunt them. It was especially galling to remember that the Tenochas had once served as mercenaries of the Tepanecs. For these reasons, Itzcoatl ordered the old chronicles of the state archive destroyed and replaced by a new "official history," which emphasized the Aztecs' role as the chosen people of Huitzilopochtli. The Tepanecs were portrayed as barbarian oppressors, and the role of the Texcocans was downplayed.

The rewriting of Aztec history had bloody consequences. Although the Aztecs were more warlike and aggressive than some of their contemporaries, they previously had not differed substantially in their customs and religious beliefs. Now, however, as the Aztecs sought to assert their superiority, human sacrifice was elevated to a central role in society. Mass human sacrifices were a weapon of terror, designed to strike fear into the hearts of Tenochtitlán's enemies. At the same time, such sacrifices served to convince the Aztec people that their gods demanded constant warfare. To some extent, the new policy was the creation of Tlacaelel, who used the rewritten histories to secure his own position and to justify his war policies. Tlacaelel remained the driving force of Aztec society for more than half a century, honored as the epitome of religious and martial virtues until his death during the reign of Ahuitzotl.

Said to be a pleasure-loving man who cared more for women and good food than for war, Ahuitzotl nevertheless presided over the last great era of Aztec conquest. At the time of his death in 1503, Tenochtitlán's power was at its height and the strains of empire were beginning to show. The era of expansionism had lasted just over a century and made the Tenochas masters of more than five million subjects. The "empire," though, was essentially an overgrown city-state. Although their domains extended outward from the Central Plateau of Mexico to include lands from Guatemala to the northern deserts, the Aztecs showed little desire to settle beyond the crowded islands of Lake Texcoco.

Like Venice, Tenochtitlán of the early sixteenth century was a city of canals, bridges, dikes, and em-

Above, the lid of a terra-cotta censer from Teotihuacán, dating from about the fifth century A.D. Below, the Aztec Calendar Stone, in the heart of Tenochtitlán. The face in the center of the stone is thought to be that of Tonatiuh, the sun god. This Eagle Knight (right) wears the helmet characteristic of his order.

The Feathered Serpent and The Cross

Hernando Cortés (below) had hoped to add Tenochtitlán to the domains of Emperor Charles V of Spain. With the help of Manliche, the Nahua-speaking woman who served as his interpreter, he nearly succeeded in conquering the Aztecs by guile.

48

Above, Spanish ships.

Left, a sixteenth-century Portuguese map showing Central and South America.

bankments. Its setting, in the center of a blue lake on a plateau ringed by tall mountains, could not have been more dramatic. The impression of a fairy-tale city—"like the enchantments they tell of in the legend of Amadis," according to the sixteenth-century Spanish soldier and historian Bernal Díaz del Castillo—was enhanced by the inhabitants' custom of plastering their single-storied adobe houses a gleaming white and by the profusion of chinampas, which were planted with ornamental flowers as well as vegetables and corn.

Three broad causeways, each eight yards wide, connected the island city, on which the main temple and the palace of the Aztecs were located, to the mainland. Two of the causeways were provided with aqueducts that carried fresh water into the city, and all were pierced at intervals with channels that allowed free passage to water traffic. These channels were spanned by portable wooden bridges that could be quickly moved in case of attack.

At the center of the city lay the sacred precinct, whose many temples towered over the private houses of the surrounding districts. Here too was the royal palace, which contained quarters for Montezuma's two wives and numerous concubines, storehouses for the royal treasures, and the king's private zoo and aviary.

It is estimated that in 1519, when a Spanish force led by Hernando Cortés entered the city, Tenochtitlán had as many as 200,000 inhabitants. If so, it was easily as large as any European capital of the day. Little wonder that Cortés wrote to the emperor Charles V that the Tenochas "live almost as we do in Spain, with quite as much orderliness." In more candid moments, the Spanish conquerors admitted that Tenochtitlán was in some respects more advanced than the cities they had known in Europe. They were amazed to discover, for example, that the city was provided with public latrines in the form of small boats that were conveniently docked near busy walkways and discreetly shielded by reed screens from the view of passers-by.

The masters of this great city bore little resemblance to the impoverished wanderers who had arrived at Lake Texcoco almost two centuries before. The rise to empire had transformed a simple and generally egalitarian society into one that was highly conscious of the benefits of rank. The *calpulli*, a clanlike extended family, remained the basic unit of Aztec social life, but the custom of electing clan leaders had gradually faded. Officials, who were chosen from a single small group of ruling families, gradually became less accountable to the people and more accountable to the king. Traditionally the Aztec emperor was also elected, but by the time Montezuma II reached the throne the only eligible candidates were members of the reigning family and the number of electors had shrunk to four.

For the average Aztec, the usual pathway to distinction was through warfare. Virtually every Aztec male was destined to see battle at one time or another, and all—except for those who trained for the priesthood—spent several years of their lives in communal "houses of the young men," where they were educated in the martial arts. Upon emerging from one of these schools, a young man wore his hair in a distinctive cut, with a single long lock left unshorn at the nape of his neck. He was not permitted to cut off this lock until he had captured his first prisoner in battle.

The great majority of these young warriors in time retired from fighting to become farmers. But those who were lucky or valiant enough to capture many prisoners earned the right to join the ranks of the professional soldiers. For the most illustrious, promotion might eventually lead to membership in the elite ranks of the Jaguar or Eagle Knights. Such warriors fought for glory as much as for wealth and were the heroes of the state, universally admired and singled out for special honors on ceremonial occasions.

Although Aztec women could not be warriors, their lives too were dominated by the demands of the military state, because to fill the ranks of the army a high birthrate was essential. Girls were usually married at sixteen, in a ceremony that involved literally "tying the knot"—the bride's blouse was joined with the groom's cloak. A wife had certain rights, including the right to own property, but sterility was grounds for summary divorce.

The lives of most women revolved around the daily preparation of corn, a laborious process that involved soaking the corn in limewater, partially cooking the corn to loosen the hard outer kernels, grinding the flour, and shaping and cooking the tortillas. Tortillas and tamales—the latter filled with everything from squash blossoms and peppers to salamanders and grubs—had to be prepared daily. This time-consuming duty, along with weaving, helping in the fields, and, in time of war, carrying supplies for armies on the move, must have left little time for leisure.

The wives and concubines of important men were rich enough to cultivate a vogue for simplicity. Well-bred Aztec women considered beauty aids déclassé. Such cosmetics as yellow cream for the complexion and red dye for the teeth were used mostly by courtesans assigned to serve the soldiers. They must have tempted respectable girls, however, for it was necessary for fathers to warn their daughters against them.

Left, Aztec rites as depicted by an Indian artist after the Spanish conquest. The Spanish historian and missionary Bernardino de Sahagún commissioned these drawings in the mid-sixteenth century; they did not become widely known, however, until 1905. This detail (above) shows young warriors preparing to climb a pole as part of a ceremony. Right, an illustration from a sixteenth-century manuscript, with annotations by a Spanish scholar. Aztec scribes kept voluminous records of tribute payments, landholdings, lawsuits, and other civil and religious matters.

These drawings from the Codex Osuna (1565) show work being done by Indians (center left) for colonial officials (near left). The digging stick, held by the worker in the upper right of the Indian scene, was the most indispensable tool of agriculture before the Spanish conquest.

51

The Aztec gods

The Aztecs envisioned a complex universe divided horizontally into five regions, each inhabited by its own gods. Only a few of these deities intervened directly in human affairs. Among them were Tezcatlipoca, who was associated with night and darkness, and Quetzalcoatl, the god of knowledge and Tezcatlipoca's eternal adversary. Most other gods were remote, representing the complex rhythms of the natural forces that the Aztecs sought to propitiate.

The Aztecs' acute awareness of the violence and uncertainty of the world around them led them to attribute many fearful characterisitics to their deities: Xipe, the god of planting, was portrayed wearing a suit of flayed human skin, and Coatlicue, the earth goddess, was shown with a necklace of human hands draped around her shoulders. To apprehend the intentions of their gods, the Aztecs relied on ritual, sorcery, and fortunetelling. Religion was ceremonial and had little to do with individual behavior or morality.

Below, Xiuhtecuhtli, one of the most ancient and important Mexican gods, who was identified with the life-giving warmth of fire. This coiled feathered serpent (right) represents Quetzalcoatl, a kind of "supergod" at the time of the Spanish conquest.

Huehuetéotl (above), the "old, old god," was a fire divinity and the protector of the hearth. Above right, a Tlaloque, or assistant of Tlaloc, the rain god, emptying water and corn from a precious stone vessel. Chalchiuhtlicue, or Green Stone Skirt (right), presided over the welfare of lakes and rivers.

This fearsome mask (left), fashioned from a human skull, depicts Tezcatlipoca, a god who was ever young, omnipotent, omnipresent, and omniscient. The mask is inlaid with bands of turquoise and lignite and is fitted out with pyrite eyes. Tezcatlipoca, who was associated with darkness, the night, and the jaguar, was the eternal rival of Quetzalcoatl, the civilizing god.

"Listen to me, child," reads one text. "Never make up your face nor paint it, never put red on your mouth to look beautiful. Makeup and paint are things that light women use—shameless creatures. If you want your husband to love you, dress well, wash yourself and wash your clothes."

In theory, all Aztec men were soldiers, farmers, priests, officials, slaves, or *tolteca*—goldsmiths, jewelers, painters, and featherworkers. Yet there was another rising class within Aztec society: the *pochteca,* or merchants, who were responsible for supplying the markets of central Mexico with luxury goods from distant lands. The pochteca were quite wealthy and were divided into many distinct ranks, each of which jealously guarded its special privileges with regard to dress and lifestyle. These merchants, who devoted their lives to the acquisition of riches rather than to warfare and religious duties, seem to have aroused a good deal of resentment. Wealthy as they were, the pochteca took great pains to appear poor, wearing worn-out cloaks in public and hiding their goods in secret warehouses.

The wealth and power of Tenochtitlán was built on two centuries of unremitting but by no means unregulated warfare. Potential enemies were duly warned in advance and given ample chance to surrender before actual hostilities began, and war was never declared without some provocation being cited.

Once a given war ended, there was no thought of assimilating the conquered enemy. The goal of Aztec statecraft was tribute, pure and simple. Wherever possible, provincial governors preferred to work through the existing power structure. Throughout the empire the most visible representative of the Aztec presence was the *calpixque,* or tax collector.

Soon after their arrival on the eastern coast of Mexico, Cortés and his soldiers had occasion to witness the arrival of a party of tax gatherers in a Totoanac village. According to a vivid description by

Above, Aztec warriors besieging Alvarado and his men in their palace garrison. One of the warriors wears the feathered costume of an Eagle Knight. Right, a detail of a quetzal-feather and gold headdress. A gift of Montezuma II to Cortés, the headdress was later presented to Emperor Charles V of Spain.

Díaz del Castillo, news of the arrival of five Mexican (Aztec) officials left the villagers "trembling with fear." "Very quickly, they decorated a room with flowers and cooked them some food, and made great quantities of chocolate. . . ." When the calpixques entered the town, added Díaz, they walked with "cocksure pride . . . speaking not a word to Cortés or to anyone else they saw. They wore richly embroidered cloaks and loincloths . . . and [had] shining hair that was gathered up and seemed to be tied to their heads. Each one was smelling the roses that he carried."

The most onerous element of the tribute system was represented by the Aztecs' continual demands for human captives to serve as sacrifices for the gods. One scholar has estimated that by the late fifteenth century as many as 250,000 victims were slain each year

Daily life among the Aztecs

Drawings made by native artists and used as illustrations for books by early Spanish ethnographers have greatly enriched our knowledge of daily life among the Aztecs. A great number of these pictures concern the planting, harvesting, and storage of corn—activities that occupied many of the working hours of Aztec farmers. The daily routine of women was dominated by the preparation of corn for the table, but their tasks were less often portrayed in the early sources.

Among the Aztecs, urban occupations enjoyed greater prestige than farming. Especially high status was assigned to such craftsmen as featherworkers, goldsmiths, and stone carvers. Because urban occupations were restricted to members of kin groups known as *calpulli*, the crafts were generally hereditary.

These pages, illustrations from Bernardino de Sahagún's General History. *Above right, an Aztec goldsmith at work. Below, cremation of an Aztec corpse. Before cremation, the bodies of those who died a natural death were elaborately prepared for the arduous journey through the underworld.*

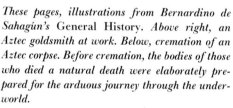

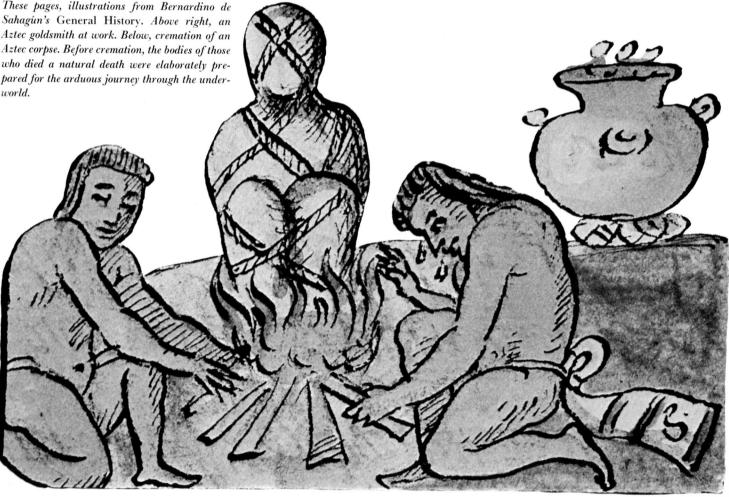

Above, the corn harvest. Above right, Aztec stone-cutters preparing building blocks for a Christian church. Right, filling storage bins with corn. Featherworkers (below) were among the most respected Aztec craftsmen. They fashioned cloaks and banners from whole plumes knotted together and made "mosaics" from bits of colored feathers glued to stiffened cloth backgrounds.

San Agustín

Of the many enigmas of pre-Incan civilization, few are as tantalizing as that of San Agustín. This cluster of sites on the Magdalena River in Colombia contains the remnants of a culture that flourished from the last centuries before Christ until after the coming of the Spaniards. San Agustín is notable for its slab chambers covered with earth mounds, its deep grave shafts, its rock-cut tombs, and—most especially— its monolithic statues, many with flaring nostrils and fanglike incisors. Speculation has linked these works with many peoples, including the Olmecs of Mexico, but their creators were probably related to a cult of feline worshipers that became widespread in Peru before 800 B.C.

This page, a selection of San Agustin figures in a variety of anthropomorphic forms.

Some groupings of San Agustin monoliths (facing page, above and below) support thin slab roofs.

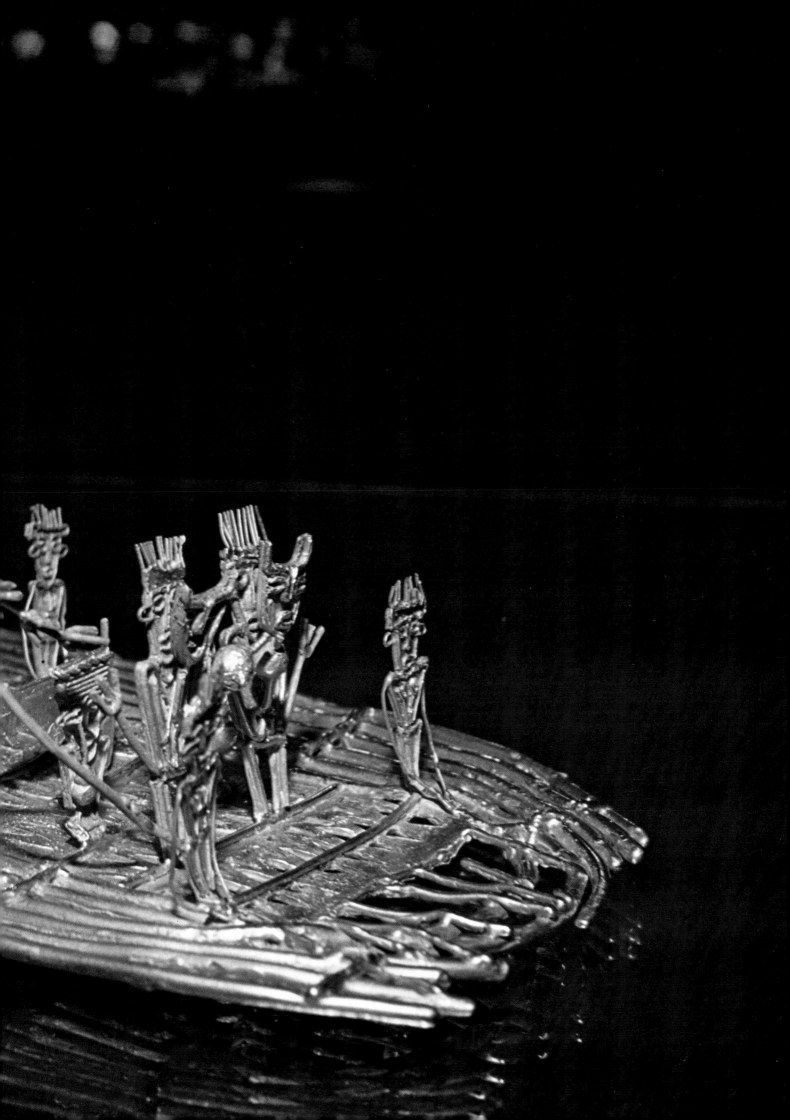

Preceding pages, a king and his attendants sailing on a golden raft. This artifact from Colombia recalls an annual rite in which the local ruler, covered from head to toe with gold dust, threw emeralds and gold nuggets into Lake Guatavita. Exaggerated reports of the wealth of this region led many Europeans to believe that the fabled land of El Dorado had at last been found.

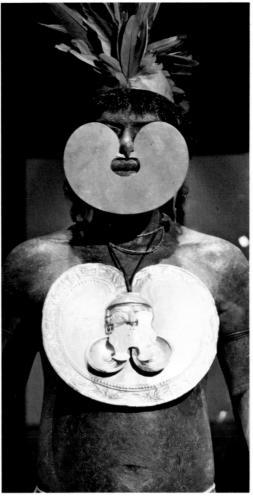

The gold of El Dorado

As the metal whose luster reflected the glory of the sun god, gold was valued by the Incas for religious as well as aesthetic reasons. These pages, a selection of pre-Columbian artifacts from the collection of the Gold Museum in Bogotá suggesting the range of uses for gold.

With few exceptions, the works of pre-Columbian goldsmiths were melted down to fill the coffers of the Spanish treasury. The German artist Albrecht Dürer, who saw some of Montezuma's treasures before their destruction, commented enthusiastically: "In all my life I have never seen anything that so delighted my heart." Charles V did not share Dürer's interest in "the subtle ingenuity of these people of foreign lands," however, and the ransom for the Incan emperor Atahualpa, which was delivered to the Spaniards partly in the form of gold artifacts, was turned into ingots before it left Peru. The value of this unprecedented ransom has been estimated at $8,344,307—and this at a time when an ounce of gold was worth only $35.07. Needless to say, news of this payment fed rumors of the existence of El Dorado, the legendary kingdom rich in gold and jewels, fervently sought after by sixteenth-century explorers.

Loftier than any mountains except the Himalayas, the Andes (above) are a double chain of peaks separated by deep, habitable valleys.

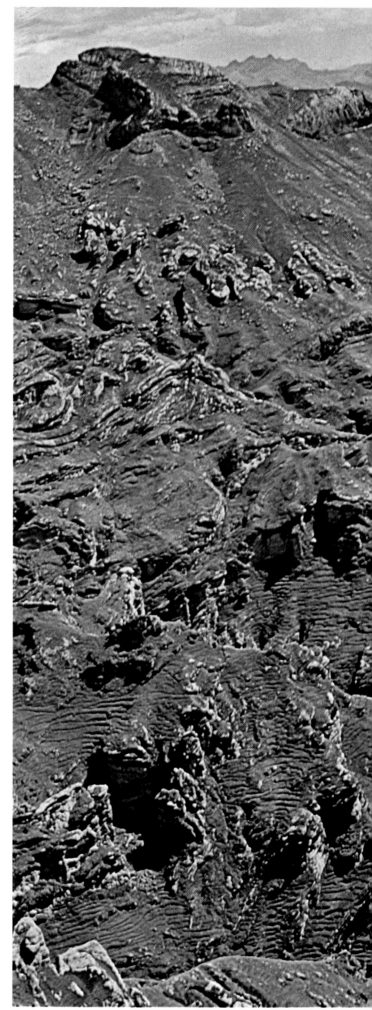

throughout the Aztecs' domains. In 1487, Ahuitzotl, the eighth and most powerful of the Aztec royal line, celebrated the dedication of the temple of Huitzilopochtli in Tenochtitlán by marshaling four lines of prisoners past teams of priests who worked four days to dispatch them. On this occasion, as many as 80,000 were slain during a single ceremonial rite.

Sacrificial rituals took many forms. For the feast of the fire god, prisoners were slowly roasted over hot coals, only to be snatched from the fire with a grappling hook and killed by a priest. On the day sacred to the goddesses of the earth, women danced, pretending ignorance of their fate, until priests crept up behind them and cut off their heads. Nevertheless, the most common form of sacrifice—and the only one ever witnessed by the Spaniards—involved stretching a male captive over a sacrifice stone while a priest ripped out his still-beating heart. The hearts were presented to the gods, and the rest was consumed by upper-class Aztecs.

Grisly as such rites may seem to us, the Aztecs viewed them as ennobling. Victims were often dressed in rich clothing, and they died in the belief that they would soon join the Sun in his heavenly paradise. No doubt many, if not all, went willingly. Ironically, the priests responsible for maintaining the cults that

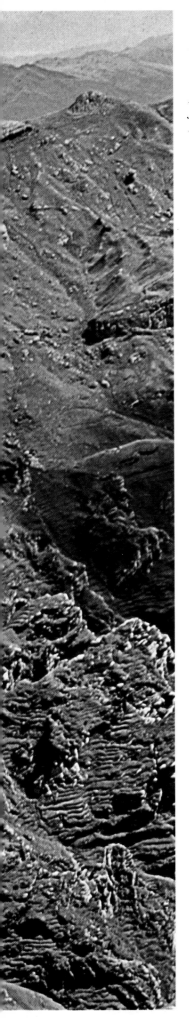

The western slopes (left) of the Andes face the coastal desert and are typically bare of trees and snow. The llama (below) was invaluable as a high-altitude pack animal. A domesticated relative of the wild guanaco, it was also prized as a source of meat, wool, and dung for fuel. The high arid plateaus of the central Andes (bottom) were the original homeland of the Quechua-speaking people.

Above, a map showing the extent of the Incan Empire.

killed so many were educated in schools dedicated to Quetzalcoatl, the god whose promised return was expected to overturn the existing order and bring an end to human sacrifice.

Given this belief in the return of Quetzalcoatl, it is not surprising that Montezuma I reacted with alarm to the portents of destruction that seemed to be everywhere in the second decade of the sixteenth century. In one particularly disturbing incident, Montezuma's huntsmen captured a strange bird with a mirror in its forehead, and when the emperor looked into the mirror he saw a host of armed men advancing on Tenochtitlán. Rumors of the appearance of unnatural monsters were reaching the capital almost daily, and not the least of these was the story that strange beasts with four legs and human torsos and heads had appeared on the coast of Tabasco.

With his excellent intelligence network, Montezuma was soon able to learn that these creatures were men on horseback, who ate, slept, and bled like anyone else. Further news of this army of fewer than four hundred Spanish adventurers was anything but encouraging, however. As Montezuma's successive attempts to rid himself of the strangers failed, it seemed the Spanish were destined to reach Tenochtitlán in accordance with the will of the gods. Montezuma therefore welcomed the Spanish force into his capital, personally escorting Cortés and his lieutenants on a tour of the city.

The first sight to dazzle the Spaniards on this tour was the great marketplace at Tlatelolco. Díaz del Castillo later wrote at length of the astounding variety of goods he saw displayed there, beginning with gold, silver, and precious stones and continuing with "slaves attached to long poles by means of collars round their necks, cotton goods, . . . sisal cloth and ropes and sandals, . . . the skins of lions and tigers, otters, jackals and deer, . . . kidney beans and sage, . . . fowls, and birds with great dewlaps, . . . honey paste and other sweets like nougat, . . . canoe loads of

Above left, a pottery figure from a pre-Incan grave of about the fifth century A.D. Left, a lacquered wooden beaker. The highly schematic decoration is typical of Incan craftsmanship during colonial times. This battle scene (right), painted on wood, was found at the Temple of the Sun in Cuzco.

human excrement (to be used for the curing of skins), . . . tobacco, . . . cochineal dye, . . . cakes made from a sort of weed which they get out of the lake and which curdles and forms a bread which tastes rather like cheese, . . . axes of bronze and copper, . . . gold dust placed in the quills of large geese of that country."

When the procession left Tlatelolco, though, and moved on to the temple that housed the twin shrines of Tlaloc and Huitzilopochtli, the amazement and admiration of the Spaniards quickly turned to horror. At the summit of the lofty pyramid were the idols of Hummingbird-on-the-Left and Smoking Mirror, each thickly encrusted with pearls and precious stones and bits of mirror glass. Five hearts, sacrificed earlier that day, were still smoking in a brazier before one of the idols. Díaz del Castillo wrote: "The walls of that shrine were so splashed and caked with blood that they and the floor too were black. Indeed, the whole place stank abominably."

Cortés' offer to replace idols with an image of the Virgin Mary met with the following response from Montezuma: "If I had known that you were going to utter these insults I should not have shown you my gods."

When the Spaniards moved to take Montezuma hostage, the Aztec ruler did not urge his courtiers to

fight on his behalf. Perhaps he was a prisoner of his fatalistic temperament or perhaps he had no realistic hope of mounting an effective defense. Because the capture of a head of state in central Mexico was usually the prelude to negotiations, Montezuma may simply have misunderstood the significance of the Spaniards' actions.

Tenochtitlán was not destined to fall without a struggle. Some time later, in the absence of Cortés, a nervous Spanish commander mistook an outdoor ceremony in honor of Huitzilopochtli for a rebellion and massacred the assembled celebrants. This brutality provoked a wave of popular feeling against the Span-

iards. The conquistadors were besieged inside their quarters, and Montezuma was killed in the confusion, either by his disgusted subjects or by the Spanish. Cortés, who had rejoined his men, barely managed a predawn escape across the causeway to Tacuba.

Only a handful of Spaniards survived the retreat with Cortés toward Tlaxcala, but there was no thought of giving up the fight. By the end of 1520, Cortés returned to Tenochtitlán accompanied by a reinforced army of some nine hundred Spaniards and a well-armed force of Tlascalan Indians. He brought sixteen brigantines that had been disassembled and transported in pieces over the mountains to be reas-

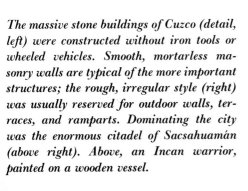

The massive stone buildings of Cuzco (detail, left) were constructed without iron tools or wheeled vehicles. Smooth, mortarless masonry walls are typical of the more important structures; the rough, irregular style (right) was usually reserved for outdoor walls, terraces, and ramparts. Dominating the city was the enormous citadel of Sacsahuamán (above right). Above, an Incan warrior, painted on a wooden vessel.

Relief carvings (top left and immediately above) from the temple at Cerro Sechín, Peru, depict an ax-wielding warrior and a trophy head. Top center, a monumental stone at Machu Picchu. Near right, a pre-Incan flask. Below, a pre-Incan painted textile fragment. Above far right, a column of the Temple of Viracocha near Cuzco. Below far right, part of the Tampu Machay, a sanctuary whose holy springs were believed to possess healing powers.

sembled on the shores of Lake Texcoco.

In the assault on Tenochtitlán, Cortés and his soldiers conducted a kind of campaign that was just as horrifying to the Aztecs as the Aztecs' sacrifices were to the Spanish: They waged war against the whole population of the city. The besiegers of Tenochtitlán cut off the water supply, embargoed all food deliveries, and leveled whole neighborhoods. Although without allies, the Aztecs fought bravely under the resolute leadership of Cuauhtemoc, Montezuma's nephew.

In August 1521, Cuauhtemoc was finally forced to yield. The once gleaming and immaculate city of Tenochtitlán was now filled with the stench of death, and the survivors begged permission to evacuate. "For three whole days," wrote Díaz del Castillo, "they streamed out of the city and all three causeways were crowded with men, women and children so thin, sallow, dirty and stinking that it was pitiful to see them. We found the houses full of corpses."

Eight years later, Cortés presented himself at the court of Emperor Charles V in Toledo, where he was appointed marquis of the Valley of Oaxaca, a title that carried with it vast tracts of land in south-central Mexico and an income surpassing that of any marquis in Spain. For the aging conquistador, who had hoped to become governor of New Spain, the honor was something of a disappointment. However, he was still willing to approach the emperor on behalf of an obscure fellow colonist, Francisco Pizarro, who was seeking support for a new venture on the Pacific coast of South America. Thanks partly to Cortés' backing, Pizarro was named governor general of Peru—the land of the Incas.

In 1526—five years after the fall of Tenochtitlán—Huayna Capac, the eleventh emperor of the Incas, was holding court at his palace in Tumibamba when messengers from the coast reported the arrival of a party of "curious strangers" on the beach of Tumbéz. "Their faces were white and they had beards and were covered from head to foot in clothing, and they were altogether quite wild in their appearance . . . [and they] had crossed the seas in great wooden houses," the messengers related. Huayna Capac's reaction was extreme. "The Inca was speechless at what he heard and was overcome by such melancholy and dismay that he retired to his chamber and did not emerge until the darkness had begun to fall."

Although this description was not set down until a century after the event, there is good reason to suppose that the report of Huayna Capac's distress was by no means exaggerated. After several centuries of aggressive expansion, the empire of the Incas had just

Lake Titicaca

High in the Andes, thirteen miles from the southeastern shore of Lake Titicaca, stands Tiahuanaco, a ceremonial center with impressive masonry buildings and stylized human statues in red sandstone. The Incas were aware of the grandeur of this vanished civilization and associated the Titicaca region with their own origins. One late version of the Incan creation myth places the first home of Manco Capac and Mama Occla—ancestors of the Incan people—on an island in the lake's center. In reality, the Titicaca basin did not come under Incan control until the reign of the fifteenth-century emperor Viracocha. Like the area's inhabitants at that time, the people of this region today earn their living by fishing with nets from balsa rafts.

At 12,500 feet above sea level, Lake Titicaca (above) is the world's highest navigable body of water. The lake has no major outlets but drains into a marshy area (below and near right) that extends southward from the Bolivian shore.

Below, the ruins of a small temple on one of Titicaca's small islands. Legend associated this shrine with Manco Capac and Mama Occla, ancestors of the Incan people.

The celebrated balsa rafts of Titicaca (immediately above and above right) are fashioned from tightly woven bunches of reeds. The crafts' resemblance to the papyrus-reed boats of the ancient Egyptians has inspired many fanciful theories; serious scholars are convinced, however, that the techniques evolved independently.

Left, a stone ceremonial vase. Immediately below, the foundations of a circular building at Sacsahuamán; much of the fortress was dismantled by the Spaniards. Right, a stone to which, according to one interpretation, Incan priests ritually "tied" the sun. This face of a present-day Quechua Indian (bottom left) bears a striking resemblance to this anthropomorphic vase (bottom right) from the Incan period.

entered a new and troubled era. Its conquering armies had pushed north and east to the edge of the tropical rain forest, territory that the Incas found hostile and forbidding. In the south, there were rumors that a lowlands people from the Río Platte area were moving into Incan lands on the Bolivian *altiplano*. In Cuzco, the Incas' capital, there were rumblings of discontent, and some disgruntled aristocrats spoke openly about the prophecy that Huayna Capac's line would produce only twelve rulers and that the next Inca was thus fated to preside over the demise of the empire. Worst of all, the realm of the Incas had for the previous twelve years been visited by outbreaks of a mysterious plague that decimated and demoralized the army, swept through several provinces, and wreaked havoc in the capital. Huayna Capac had no way of knowing that his most serious and immediate problems—both the plague and the invasion from the Río Platte—were caused by the arrival of Europeans.

Like the Aztecs, the Incas were latecomers on the stage of history, aggressive militarists who had subjugated their neighbors and were vulnerable to revolt from within. Both cultures also believed that they had learned the civilized arts from a creator god whose return was promised in legend. Unlike any of the peoples of Mesoamerica, however, the Incas were able to develop the centralized administration associated with a fully matured imperial state. An absolute ruler, the Lord Inca (emperor) stood at the summit of a consummately organized political machine—one with clear lines of authority running from the village headmen on the local level to the provincial governors (who were members of a hereditary ruling class) to the Lord Inca himself.

Every married male in the Incan Empire was enrolled as a taxpayer, and in return for contributing his labor to the state he was guaranteed complete security. There was no such thing as unemployment; if jobs were not available, the state created them. Widows and orphans were assured support, and the food supply was stabilized by a system of state gran-

Incan burial customs

The ancient Peruvians considered the dead and the places associated with them to be *huaca*—a term applied to objects believed to have holy or magic powers. All families who could afford to do so made special arrangements for their departed relatives. The bodies of the dead were wrapped in many yards of cloth bandages, provided with offerings of food and ceremonial objects, and then interred in family vaults.

The mummies of the Lord Incas and their queens received special care. The fifteenth-century Lord Inca Pacachuti went so far as to establish the custom of treating departed Lord Incas as if they were still alive. From his reign on, royal mummies were kept in the palaces where they had resided during their lifetimes, attended by corps of servants who carefully fanned away flies, prepared meals for the mummies, and carried their charges into the streets to be seen and worshiped on special occasions.

Many royal mummies were destroyed and numerous Incan tombs violated by the Spanish conquistadors in their search for hidden treasure.

Right, a mummy discovered at the Paracas Necropolis in 1925. This wood and cloth doll (below) was found at Pativilca, on the coastal plain northwest of Lima.

Peruvian Indians sometimes buried their dead in above-ground vaults. This tomb (above) is the work of Aymara Indians living in the Lake Titicaca basin. Left, the head of an Incan mummy, now in the Cuzco Archaeological Museum. Below, the face of a false head for a mummy bundle.

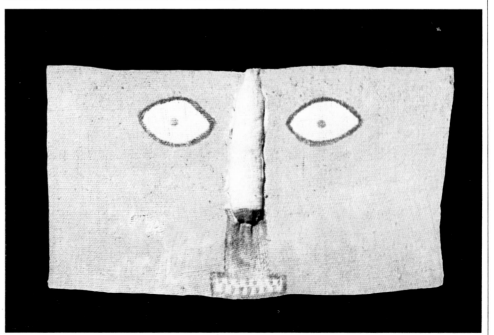

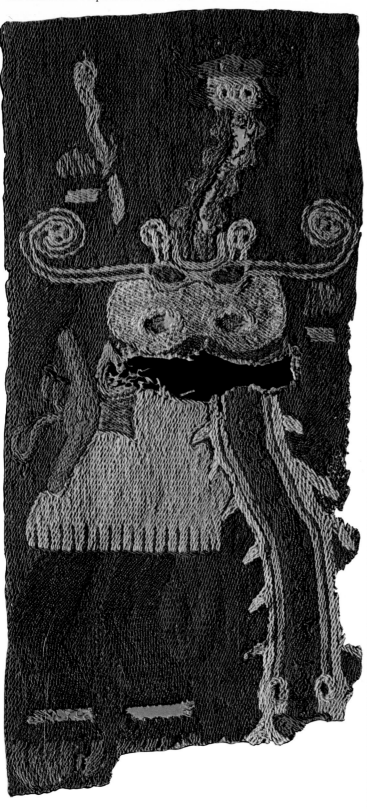

Above, detail of an embroidered textile from Paracas. Normally, designs were woven directly into the fabric. Facing page, above and below left, remains of the Incan City of Pisac in the Urubamba Valley. Pisac's stone ramparts and steep terraced hills are outstanding examples of Incan public works. Facing page, below right, a stone figure from the Central Peruvian Highlands, dating from approximately A.D. 700.

aries. In return for these benefits, though, the common householder and his family accepted an imperial authority that extended to the most routine matters of daily life.

Land in the Incan state was divided into three parts—one for the support of the Inca and his large extended family, one for the gods, and one for the community. The farmer was expected to contribute labor to the cultivation of state and religious lands as well as to serve for five years in some large-scale state enterprise, either the army, the mines, or projects to build roads or terrace hillside fields. He was not permitted to travel on private business and was obliged to marry at age twenty. His home could be entered at any time by imperial inspectors empowered to report on such matters as the quality of his wife's housekeeping.

This pre-Columbian welfare state was the creation of a people that could trace its history back no more than three centuries. The first Lord Inca, Manco Capac, was said to have emerged from a "royal window"—most likely the mouth of a cave—some time around A.D. 1200. In time, Manco Capac married his eldest sister, Mama Occlu, succeeded in eliminating his rival brothers, and conquered the fertile valley of Cuzco, "the navel of the world." This conquest, according to the most reliable of the Incan legends, established the first homeland of the Quechua-speaking people who called themselves "children of the sun" and whom we know as the Incas.

The expansion of Incan territory did not begin until the fifteenth century, when Viracocha, the eighth Lord Inca and namesake of the creator god Viracocha, came to power. Toward the end of Viracocha's reign, Cuzco was nearly conquered by a rival tribe, the Chanca. As the Inca and his chosen heir abandoned their people and barricaded themselves in a nearby fortress, one of Viracocha's other sons, Cusi Yupanqui, stayed behind to rally the war leaders for a last-ditch battle. The Chanca were defeated—an outcome so miraculous that Cusi Yupanqui later claimed that the very stones of the battlefield had sprung to life on his behalf. Acting on the mandate of this victory, Cusi Yupanqui ordered the execution of his discredited brother. In 1438 he was proclaimed Pacachuti Inca Yupanqui, the ninth ruler of the Incan people.

Pacachuti and Topa Yupanqui, his son, were energetic conquerors who have sometimes been compared with Philip II of Macedonia and his son Alexander the Great. Under their leadership, the Incas became the dominant power in the Andes region, controlling most of present-day Peru and Ecuador and large areas in what is now Bolivia, Chile, and Argentina.

Above, llama statuettes made of sheet gold. The lungs of sacrificed llamas were used for divination. Near right, a small ceramic vase. Terraced hillsides (below and far right) enabled the Incas to increase their yield of corn. Potatoes were the staple food of high-altitude dwellers; corn was grown at lower altitudes.

Many of the forms of imperial organization introduced by Pacachuti were borrowed from older Andean civilizations. Earlier peoples, such as the Tiahuanaco and the Huari, had built an extensive system of roads. The neighboring Chimú, whose capital extended over six square miles, had developed a highly structured social system. Pacachuti was able to adapt many of the technical and social accomplishments of other cultures to the needs of his new empire. His chief innovations were in the field of religion, where he reorganized existing Incan rituals to create an imperial mystique, and in warfare, where he introduced a supply system that made it possible for the Incan army to undertake large and extensive campaigns far from home.

Unlike their Mesoamerican counterparts, Incan soldiers fought to kill. Captured enemy leaders were sometimes set aside for human sacrifice, but Incan soldiers were not expected to waste their time taking live prisoners. Warriors in the front ranks of the Incan advance fought with bolas or slings, but the fighting fell in large part to foot soldiers, who carried clubs with stone or metal warheads. Once the signal for hand-to-hand combat was given, all thought of discipline vanished and the fray grew fierce.

As soon as victory was won, the Incas moved methodically to assimilate conquered lands. Teams of officials traveled through the new province conducting a census while engineers prepared a master plan for public works, including roads and irrigation systems. Conquered peoples were expected to learn the Quechua tongue and to adopt Incan dress, but they retained the characteristic headgear that set them apart from ethnic Incas. In some cases, there was forced resettlement: Quechua-speaking colonists were introduced into newly won territory to speed the process of acculturation, and potentially rebellious groups were sometimes deported to distant provinces. Defeated chieftains were recognized as a sort of secondary nobility. Although these so-called *curacas* could never become the equals of the *orejones,* or members of the native Incan ruling class, they can have had little reason to regret their submission to the Incas. Their loyalty was secured by generous gifts, and life in the Incan provinces seems generally to have been comfortable and secure.

The Incan approach to government was so efficient that many writers have been tempted to idealize the empire. Historians have sometimes described the realm of Pacachuti and Topa Yupanqui as a "utopia" that anticipated the modern socialist state in concept and surpassed it in performance. More recent evidence suggests that Incan planning did not always work so smoothly. Not all conquered peoples were readily assimilated, and the existence of private trading ventures, which theoretically had no place in the Incan system, shows that for some, at least, there were ways of by-passing the controlled economy.

At the heart of the Incan Empire was the capital at Cuzco, a city that reached its maturity under the guidance of the Inca Pacachuti. Pedro Sancho de la Hoz, one of the few Europeans to see Incan Cuzco before its destruction, called it "so beautiful that it is worthy of being seen in Spain." "It is full of lordly palaces," he added, "and there are no poor people in sight. . . . There are many houses of adobe and they are well laid out; the streets are in a checkerboard pattern and very narrow, all paved and with water channels running down the middle . . . ."

The remains of Cuzco's monumental stone temples, palaces, and walls have a somber look today, but Cuzco at its height must have been a brilliant and colorful city. The walls of the most important buildings were covered with friezes of beaten gold and silver, and thatched roofs were designed in intricate and ingenious patterns. The markets overflowed with the finest goods produced throughout the empire, and the temples were stocked with the treasures of conquered peoples. The famous Coricancha, or Sun Temple, for example, boasted a ceremonial garden "planted" with cornstalks fashioned from pure gold.

Although the wealth of empire flowed toward Cuzco, the Lord Inca was required to spend much of his reign in the provinces, where he traditionally led the army into battle seated in his golden litter and surrounded by a hand-picked bodyguard of orejones. During the reign of Huayna Capac, which began in 1493, the first signs that this situation was creating a rift between the ruler and his aristocratic subjects appeared.

The trouble began with an assault on the fortress of Caranqui in northern Ecuador, during the course of which the elite orejones suffered the first decisive defeat in their history. Worse still, Huayna Capac's

These drawings from an eighteenth-century ethnographic study depict fishermen at work and various ceremonial occasions, including festivities led by dancers in jaguar masks. Below far right, present-day mayors of villages in the Urubamba Valley dressed in traditional costumes to attend Sunday mass. Following pages, Machu Picchu, a fortified Incan city never discovered by the Spaniards of colonial times.

82

brother was killed, and the Inca himself, abandoned by his bodyguard, was unceremoniously dumped from his litter and barely escaped capture. Huayna Capac decided to punish the orejones by excluding them from the division of the campaign's spoils. As the quarrel became more bitter, he delayed his long-promised return to Cuzco and began hinting that he intended to construct a second capital in Ecuador.

This was the state of affairs in 1526, when Huayna Capac received word of Pizarro's second voyage to the New World. Not long after, the plague, which Huayna Capac had hoped to avoid by remaining in the Ecuadorian highlands, claimed the Inca as one of

its victims. Huayna Capac's death destroyed all hope of an accommodation between the nobles of Cuzco and the Inca's entourage in Ecuador. Each faction had its own candidate for the succession, the Cuzqueños favoring Huascar, who was the legitimate heir apparent, and the Ecuadorians supporting Atahualpa, the capable but arrogant son of one of Huayna Capac's minor wives. The dispute touched off an unprecedented civil war.

Fortuitously, Pizarro's next expedition made contact with the court in Ecuador just as Atahualpa was enjoying his victory over Huascar's forces. During his initial meeting with a delegation of Spaniards, Ata-

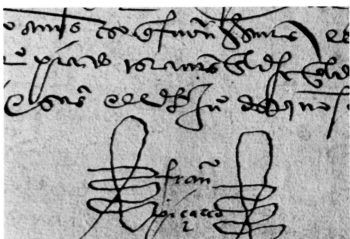

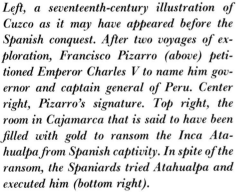

Left, a seventeenth-century illustration of Cuzco as it may have appeared before the Spanish conquest. After two voyages of exploration, Francisco Pizarro (above) petitioned Emperor Charles V to name him governor and captain general of Peru. Center right, Pizarro's signature. Top right, the room in Cajamarca that is said to have been filled with gold to ransom the Inca Atahualpa from Spanish captivity. In spite of the ransom, the Spaniards tried Atahualpa and executed him (bottom right).

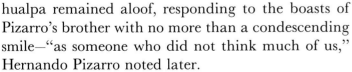

hualpa remained aloof, responding to the boasts of Pizarro's brother with no more than a condescending smile—"as someone who did not think much of us," Hernando Pizarro noted later.

The main force of the conquistadors had meanwhile occupied the nearby town of Cajamarca, where they horrified local officials by entering a house of the Chosen Women—women training to become the wives or concubines of members of the ruling class or to lead lives of celibacy in the temples—and distributing its five hundred residents among themselves. When news of this desecration reached Atahualpa, the Inca advanced toward the town with an escort of thousands. Atahualpa confidently allowed the majority of his followers to remain behind while he met with Pizarro. Then, at a prearranged signal, Spanish horsemen charged the royal litter, cutting down the bodyguard and seizing Atahualpa. The sound of firearms and the sight of their leader's capture so unnerved the Incan warriors that they gave up all thought of resistance. Hundreds were cut down as they fled, and Atahualpa was jailed. Knowing that the Spaniards were primarily interested in gold, the captive offered to buy his freedom by filling his cell with gold treasures. Although this ransom was paid, Atahualpa was nevertheless tried on a trumped-up charge of fomenting a rebellion and garroted.

The burden of the Spanish conquest fell heaviest on the common people. Disruption of the economic system, the introduction of European diseases, and the burdens of forced labor imposed by the new masters of Peru led to a disastrous decline in the birthrate. The depopulation of the once thriving empire was so dramatic that many Spaniards feared that they would soon have no subjects to rule. As the glow of New World gold dimmed and the impact of the Spanish presence became clear, there were many who questioned the course that had been taken. Among the most incisive observers was Fernando de Aemellones, who wrote in 1555: "We cannot conceal the great paradox that a barbarian like Huayna Capac kept such excellent order that the entire country was calm and all were well nourished, whereas today we see only infinite deserted villages on all the roads of the kingdom." By this point, however, there was no turning back. The last of the American Sun Kingdoms had been extinguished and the era of the Cross had begun.

The Papal States

There is no lack of dramatic incident in the history of the papacy, particularly in the early days of the Church. The Christian leaders of the infant Church were, in a sense, minority heroes who reconciled themselves to the possibility of meeting death by crucifixion or enduring a lifetime of servitude, torture, or exile. Persecuted by the state, members of the early Christian communities were often forced to live in catacombs, underground tunnels that also served as cemeteries. From these uncertain beginnings grew an institution that was, at selected moments in history, to wield supreme spiritual and temporal authority throughout the world.

Peter, whose name stands at the head of a list of

Preceding page, the interior of St. Peter's Basilica in the Vatican.

Christians adapted classical Roman buildings for their own uses. The sixth-century church of Santa Maria Antiqua (below) was built within a structure that may have been the library of the temple of Augustus at Rome. This portrait (right) of the first pope, Saint Peter, comes from Aquileia, an ancient diocese near what is now the city of Venice.

more than 270 popes, is certainly a historical figure, for there is undeniable proof of his existence and his preaching, but as far as the foundation of the Church of Rome is concerned, he is less a person than a symbol. "You are Peter," Jesus had said to the chief of his Apostles, "and on this rock I shall build my church and the powers of death shall not prevail against it. I will give you the keys to the Kingdom of Heaven and whatever you bind on Earth shall be bound in Heaven and whatever you loose on Earth shall be loosed in Heaven." The entire apostolic foundation of the Christian Church rests on these few lines. An early tradition has it that Peter, whose name means rock in Greek, was singled out by Jesus and entrusted with a pre-eminent role as the first leader of the Church in Rome. Every pope since Peter claims to be his successor and to have inherited his evangelical mission.

"Lo, I am with you always," Christ commanded his Apostles. Within decades of Christ's crucifixion, the first leaders of the Church were spreading his Word among the polyglot communities in Rome and the outlying provinces. These early converts were notable for their piety, their courage, and their fortitude—all essential qualities for the survival of the Church in the first three centuries of its history.

At first, the Christians were merely an annoyance to the Roman state. They were not respectful of civic celebrations honoring Roman pagan gods. They refused to pay homage to the emperor—who personified unity and order in the empire. They were reluctant to serve in the imperial army. As the Christians grew more populous and the fortunes of the empire declined, Roman officials increasingly viewed them as a threat to imperial order. By the end of the first century, there were settlements of Christians at Ephesus in the Asian province, at Corinth and Philippi in Greece, and even in the heart of Rome itself—sufficient numbers to provide the emperor Nero with a "vast multitude" of Christian scapegoats after a fire swept the city in A.D. 64.

Sporadic persecutions of the Christians were to continue into the fourth century. Some Christians were thrown to the lions; others had molten lead poured down their throats; still others were exiled or consigned to punitive labor in the mines. But, as one early Christian wrote, "the blood of the martyrs is the seed of the Church." Martyrs bred more martyrs, and spasmodic attempts to suppress the Christians actually strengthened the dedication of the survivors.

The lineaments of Christian faith took shape in this environment of crisis. In its first two centuries, Chris-

This bronze oil lamp (below), dating from the fifth century, symbolically depicts the Church as a boat. Steering the Church along its course are the two great Apostles of the early Christian era, Saints Peter and Paul.

Confident that they would be redeemed, Christians adorned gravestones with the symbols of their new religion. This early Christian grave stele (above) bears an inscription about the deceased and a sculpted wreath encircling the Greek letters chi and rho (X and P), the first two letters of Christ's name.

91

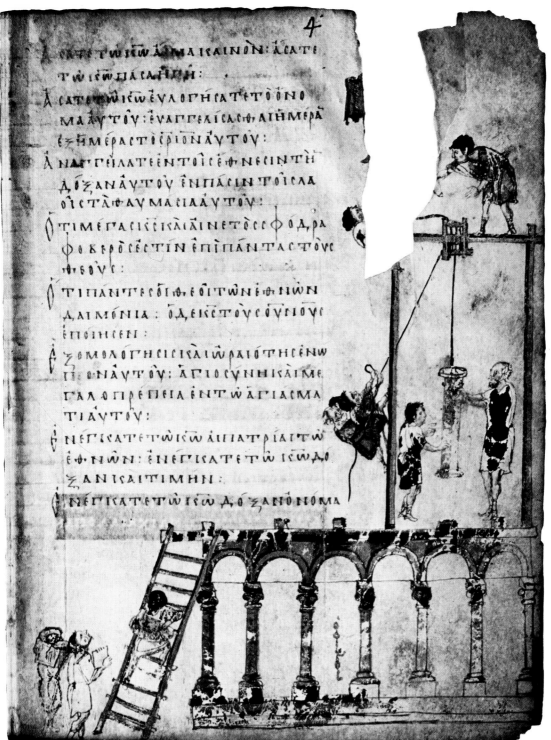

Early Christians buried their dead in catacombs (above). An early manuscript illumination (left) shows the construction of a church. Right, the church of San Sabina. Below, a fourth-century Christian sarcophagus.

tianity was compelled to differentiate itself first from Judaism and later from a Christian sect known as Gnosticism. Because the teachings of Jesus were known only through the oral tradition, they were subject to frequent misuse and misinterpretation. This danger was particularly apparent in the cities of the Eastern empire, where people mingled freely in the streets and marketplaces, spreading unorthodoxy as well as Gospel hope.

In the West, efforts to resolve doctrinal confusions were in evidence as early as A.D. 96, when Clement of Rome wrote to warn the Christians of Corinth to cease their disputes. There is a divinely appointed order to the universe, Clement told them, in which each member of the Church has a place. At the heart of this order was the authority of the bishops, who succeeded in unbroken order from the twelve Apostles chosen by Christ. Clement also implied that Rome, as the heir of Peter's mission, might have a special place. This suggestion became doctrine in the writings of Saint Irenaeus, who taught in A.D. 185 that Christ had appointed the Apostles who, in turn, appointed bishops of major cities thus ensuring an unbroken succession of Apostolic leaders in the Church. Given these precedents, it is not surprising that the word *papa* (pope)—used for all important bishops in the early days of the Church—came to be used exclusively by the bishop of Rome.

Constantine was the first emperor to perceive that the prolonged resistance of the Christians to the pagan foundation of the Roman state was a reservoir of popular strength that could be turned to the advantage of the empire. His first act in 312 was to remove all penalties against Christians. Christianity was from that time on not only tolerated but championed by the emperor himself, who converted to Christianity just before his death.

After the Council of Nicaea in 325, when Constantine formally recognized Pope Sylvester as head of all the churches in the West and liquidated the heresies then troubling the empire, Constantine retired to Constantinople and left the pope as the supreme au-

Following pages, a fresco in a thirteenth-century chapel representing the Donation of Constantine. According to legend, Constantine was cured of leprosy by Pope Sylvester I. In gratitude the emperor left Rome and gave the city forever to the pope and his heirs. In this depiction, Constantine, dressed in imperial robes, kneels before the papal throne and gratefully offers a crown to the pope, whose hand is raised in blessing.

In The City of God, *Saint Augustine proclaimed that the fall of the Roman Empire coincided with the rise of the Christian Church, the clearest earthly manifestation of the City of God. In this illustration (above) from a medieval manuscript, the saint's disciples are shown beneath churches representing the City of God.*

thority—both civil and spiritual—in Rome. The partnership of church and state *(harmonia, symphōnia)* inaugurated by Constantine was the theoretical basis for a Christian state that would continue until the fall of Constantinople in 1453.

The alliance of church and state was, in practice, uneasy from the start. Though the Church welcomed the protection Constantine offered, it warned him that the religious authorities would determine whether he behaved in an appropriately Christian way. The Church, therefore, would judge the actions of the state, yet the only way the Church could support such judgments was by political means. Herein

lies the essential dilemma of papal power—a spiritual authority dependent on political weapons. The ambiguity of this duality was fraught with hazard, not only in the time of Constantine but for centuries thereafter.

At the close of the fourth century, the Roman empire was critically undermined by the advance of the barbarians. With the disintegration of the empire came the decline of the administrative and civic organization of the state. As conditions deteriorated in the West, it became evident that the only institution capable of protecting classical civilization was the Church. So it was that churchmen took on civic duties in their dioceses, and the Church of Rome had frequent occasion to assume a leading role in confrontations with barbarians in Italy.

In this time of political anarchy, the papacy gradually consolidated its power. Pope Innocent I (pope 402–417) reaffirmed for the Roman Church the authority of the apostolic succession. In 452, Pope Leo I

marched unarmed to confront Attila, king of the Huns, who was preparing to take Rome. We can only speculate about what passed between the pacific pope and the belligerent king, but Attila agreed to cease his hostilities and spare Rome.

This now-legendary encounter points to the emergent authority of the Church—and the powerlessness of the emperor Valentinian III, who had no voice in the negotiations. For the first time, the pope had united the role of shepherd of the flock and representative of Rome and Western Europe.

By the end of the fifth century, Gelasius (pope 492–496) had sufficient confidence in his temporal

The monastic world

Monasticism played an important role in building the papal empire. Early in the sixth century an Italian monk named Benedict founded a community of monks at Monte Cassino and formulated a strict set of guidelines for his disciples to follow. The brothers were to lead simple, pious, and useful lives. They worked tilling their own land and eventually became completely self-sustaining.

Hundreds of Benedictine monasteries were established throughout Europe. Everywhere they fostered the civilized values of peace and learning and taught the useful skills of agriculture. Much of European civilization was built on foundations laid down by the monasteries, and hundreds of European towns and cities grew up in their shadows. In almost all European countries, Benedictine monasteries and nunneries worked to advance Christian ideals.

This illumination (left) from a medieval manuscript shows Saint Benedict—with an angel whispering into his ear—handing a copy of his rule to an abbot. Both Benedict and the abbot wear monastic hoods, but the saint's hood is surrounded with a golden halo. Below, the original grant given to Benedict by Pope Victor II, permitting Benedict to consecrate a church at the abbey of Monte Cassino. Within the round papal seal are a cross and the names of Jesus Christ and the Apostles Peter and Paul.

The great abbey of Monte Cassino (above) in the Apennines southeast of Rome began with a few small buildings and grew to encompass a large area. At Monte Cassino monks rose long before dawn to begin a day spent in prayer, meditation, study, and manual labor. The monks had only one meal each day. Sundays were entirely devoted to prayer.

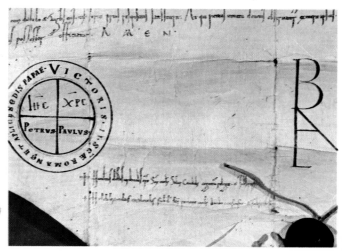

Monks were skilled in copying and illuminating ancient manuscripts. The labors of Benedictines and others preserved for posterity many literary classics that might otherwise have disappeared. Right, an illustration from a sixteenth-century manuscript. Benedict cared about literacy only because he wanted monks to read holy books. Other monastic leaders, however, fostered real scholarship and built up fine libraries.

This church (below left) in the small Italian town of Farfa, some twenty-five miles north of Rome, was originally the chapel of a Benedictine abbey. The abbot of Farfa, like many other monastic leaders, played a major role in both secular and church government and was often in Rome or at the court of a ruler.

In convents, Benedictine nuns observed basically the same rules as monks did, devoting their time to both labor and religion. This sixteenth-century illustration (right) from a copy of Benedict's rule depicts a group of nuns working in the kitchen of their nunnery beneath an image of Christ. Nuns, like monks, copied and illustrated manuscripts. Especially in England, they were famous for their handwork and for the church vestments they wove, as well as for the schools they founded for young girls.

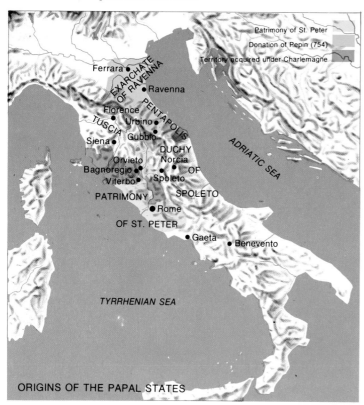

ORIGINS OF THE PAPAL STATES

THE PAPAL STATES
IN THE FOURTEENTH CENTURY

The Church in the temporal realm

The ambiguous alliance of temporal and spiritual power in the Christian Church and the frequently bitter conflicts between church and state played an ultimate role in shaping the territorial jurisdiction of the papacy. In the first 250 years, Christianity was alternately tolerated and suppressed by the Roman state. It was only in the time of the emperor Constantine that Christianity was granted official toleration in the Edict of Milan (313). Even so, the doctrinal and ecclesiastic structure of the Church evolved rather slowly, hindered by localism, heresy, and rivalries between Byzantium and the Church of Rome.

With the demise of the Roman Empire in the fifth century, the popes at Rome gradually assumed many of the temporal powers formerly exer-cised by the Western emperors. The ascendant role of the papacy in converting barbarian invaders greatly extended the geographical and spiritual influence of the Church, and gifts from converts enriched its coffers. By the eighth century, endowments of land around Rome, as well as in other parts of Italy, Sicily, and Sardinia had come to be known as the Patrimony of St. Peter.

In 754, the newly crowned Frankish ruler Pepin the Short gave the exarchate of Ravenna to Pope Stephen II in gratitude for the pope's cooperation in his coronation. This gift, the Donation of Pepin, gave succeeding popes the right to claim temporal authority over lands in central Italy, later called the Papal States. Pepin's legendary son Charles (Charlemagne) waged fifty-three campaigns in pursuit of his overriding goal—the unification of the Germanic tribes of western Europe into a cohesive Christian state.

The centuries immediately following the reign of Charles were perilous for the Church. The popes invariably became embroiled in the politics of their time, and the struggles of church and state intensified: Although Western Christendom acknowledged the pope's supremacy in the spiritual realm, its secular authority was far from secure.

Indeed, the Church's involvement in the political ambitions of competing monarchs tended to undermine its effectiveness as a spiritual authority, and abuses existed on all levels of the Church. In response, one of the Church's greatest popes, Gregory VII, worked successfully to abolish lay investiture, clerical marriage, and simony.

Gregory's uncompromising stand on lay investiture brought him into direct conflict

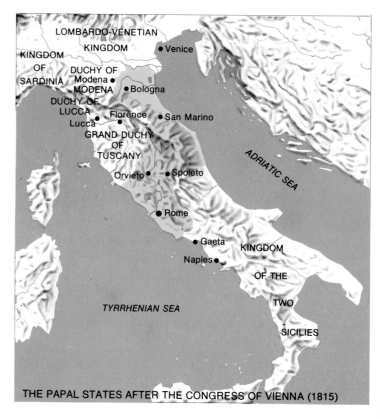

THE PAPAL STATES AFTER THE CONGRESS OF VIENNA (1815)

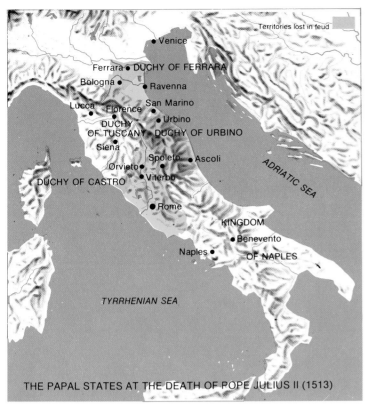

THE PAPAL STATES AT THE DEATH OF POPE JULIUS II (1513)

THE PAPAL STATES IN THE NAPOLEONIC AGE

with the Holy Roman emperor Henry IV, whom he excommunicated. Despite the drama of Henry's expedient penitance and readmission to the Church, the battle over lay investiture dragged on until a compromise settlement was reached in the Concordat of Worms (1122).

Nevertheless, contests between princes and popes continued, culminating in the Babylonian Captivity of the popes at Avignon (1309–1377). During most of the fourteenth century, the Church's effective control over its lands vacillated with its fortunes.

The Italian Renaissance posed new threats to the Church. The rise of mercantilism, the secularization of scholarship, the celebration of the individual, and the nationalistic tendencies of the nobles went far to challenge the spiritual authority of the Church. Nonetheless, the Renaissance popes excelled at managing the Vatican bureaucracy and played a highly visible role in Italian politics.

During the Italian Wars, Cesare Borgia, with the encouragement of his father Pope Alexander VI, allied himself with France and subdued the cities of the Romagna, as well as many other Italian territories. His conquests eventually came under the control of Pope Julius II. An enthusiastic warrior, Julius warred against Venice and won Ravenna, Rimini, and Faenza.

Having devoted much of their best energies to statecraft and art patronage, the Renaissance popes failed to heed the cries for reform. Religious revolts swept Europe for over a century, finally ending with the Peace of Westphalia (1648). During the crisis, the Church lost many of its worshipers to Protestantism and much of its property to Protestant princes.

Although the spiritual well-being of the Church was revitalized by the Catholic Reformation, its status as a temporal power gradually diminished. By 1809, the Church could offer no effective resistance when Napoleon Bonaparte annexed the Papal States to France.

After Napoleon's downfall, the Congress of Vienna (1815) restored the Papal States to the Church and placed them under Austrian protection. In 1870, King Victor Emmanuel II of Italy seized Rome, and the Papal States became part of United Italy. Refusing to recognize the loss of temporal power, Pope Pius IX went into exile in the Vatican, a practice his successors continued until 1929. Under the terms of the Lateran Treaty, signed in February of that year, the Vatican City became a sovereign state and its independence was guaranteed by Italy. The treaty is still in effect.

Vatican City, located within Rome, is today a state of 108.7 acres and has a population of about 650. It is the official seat of government of the Roman Catholic Church.

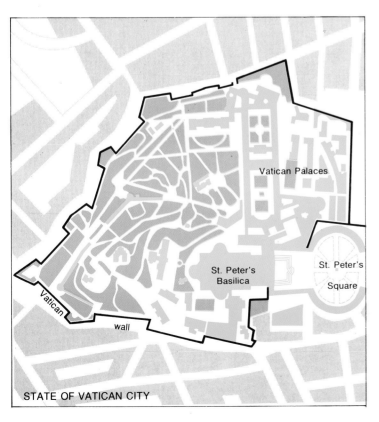

STATE OF VATICAN CITY

Vatican Palaces

St. Peter's Basilica

St. Peter's Square

Vatican wall

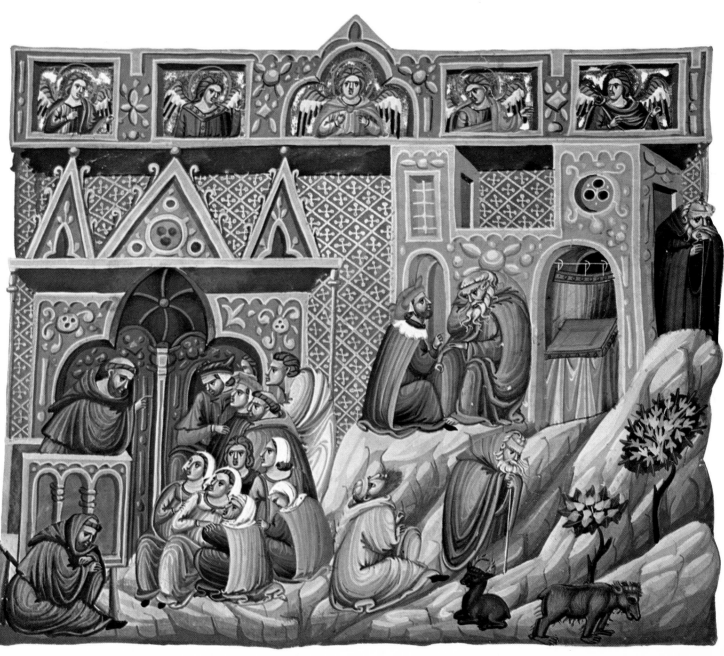

authority to write to the Eastern emperor Anastasius: "There are . . . two by whom principally this world is ruled: the sacred authority of the pontiffs and the royal power. Of these the importance of the priests is so much the greater, as even for kings of men they will have to give an account in the divine judgment."

This early period of papal growth came to fulfillment in the long pontificate of Gregory the Great (pope 590–604). The son of a Roman senator, Gregory was a consummate administrator and wise in the ways of politics and diplomacy. He sent missionaries to the farthest reaches of Europe, extending papal jurisdiction and influence with each new monastic settlement.

His corps of monks and missionaries furthered communications between the pope and the chieftains of the West, many of whom were eager to use the prestige of papal power in their bid to extend their own political authority. The pope offered these warriors the service of his monks for the privilege of converting their subjects. The wiser rulers realized they were, in fact, being offered two kingdoms, one inhabited by angels, the other by obedient subjects and extremely useful clerks and administrators.

But Gregory never let it be forgotten that the ultimate loyalty of these clerics belonged to him. The pope stressed that he was bestowing "earthly honors" on the barbarian kings. Recognition by Rome was often the sole basis on which they could compete with rivals for authority. The pope, therefore, gave assistance and advice in return for spiritual obedience. This was a precarious balance, however, possible only when the secular rulers were weak. The balance was soon upset by the rise of the powerful Frankish rulers, who held territories in the area now known as France.

Formal recognition of the developing liaisons between church and state came as early as 751, when the Frankish ruler Pepin the Short asked the pope for permission to seize the title of king from the powerless

This medieval manuscript (above left) shows monks and nuns attending mass and singing a hymn. Left, a friar preaching penitence. A pious man affected by the friar's words is seen confessing to a hermit in a rocky wilderness. Church buildings dominate the small Italian town of Sovana (top right), north of Rome. Center right, a marble chair supposedly used by Pope Gregory VII in 1084 when he consecrated the cathedral at Salerno. Bottom right, the Holy Roman emperor Henry IV pleading with Matilda, the countess of Tuscany, to intercede on his behalf with Gregory VII.

king Childeric III; Pepin was determined to rule, but he felt he needed the moral sanction of the pope. The pope's reply was succinct: "It is better that the man who has the real power should also have the title of king, rather than the man who has the mere title and no real power." With the authority of the pope behind him, Pepin gained the support of his nobles and disinvested the French king, who was "deposed, shaved, and thrust into a cloister." Pepin was now king of the Franks. The pope, too, benefited from the occasion: In the act of sanctioning the deposition of a king, he was taking precedence, symbolically at least, over all secular powers.

In return for the pope's cooperation, Pepin promised to raise an army to arrest a Lombard advance toward Rome through the exarchate of Ravenna. After two successful raids, the Franks subdued the Lombards, who promised to refrain from attacking Rome and to relinquish Ravenna and other surrounding cities. In a solemn procession, the keys to these vanquished cities were placed on Saint Peter's tomb. This gift, the Donation of Pepin, was the basis upon which the popes for centuries thereafter would claim temporal jurisdiction over central Italy. The papacy was now a temporal power, in fact and in law.

Pepin's famous son Charles, later known as Charlemagne (Charles the Great), was to inherit his father's role as protector of the papacy. At the behest of Pope Adrian, who was anxious to quell the "perfidious, stinking Lombards," Charles invaded Italy, routed their forces, and seized the Lombard crown for himself in 774. Charles was now king of the Lombards as well as of the Franks, and the papacy was heavily indebted to him.

Pope Adrian was succeeded by Pope Leo III in 795. Leo was not well liked in Rome, and soon after his accession he was beaten by a mob of armed assailants and forced to flee Rome. The pope was desperate for a protector. He might have turned to his most obvious allies—the Byzantine rulers—but they had repeatedly proved themselves useless in the struggles with the Lombards. At the time, the long-standing tensions between East and West were further complicated by irreconcilable positions in the ongoing con-

At the height of the imperial papacy, Holy Roman emperors submitted to the popes reluctantly—when they submitted at all. This fresco (left) from Siena shows a red-bearded emperor, presumably Frederick Barbarossa, in a formal act of submission before the pope.

God's servants

DOMINICHINI

42

The monastic movement resulted in the founding of numerous specialized orders of monks and nuns. Most monasteries followed Saint Benedict's rule, but eventually the need to reform monastic life gave birth to new orders. Early in the tenth century, the abbey of Cluny was established in southern France. Along with its daughter monasteries, Cluny played a major role in the reformation of the Church and in the promotion of papal supremacy. Eventually, though, the Cluniac monasteries required reshaping as well. Several new orders were started in the Middle Ages, each aiming to return to the simplicity of the original church. The Cistercians became famous for bringing many wilderness areas of Europe under cultivation. The Carthusians, another order begun in the Middle Ages, took the vows of poverty, chastity, and obedience that monks of every order made and in addition maintained silence so that talk would not interfere with their religious devotions. Later, orders of mendicant friars—who went out into the world instead of withdrawing from it—were founded. One such order, the Franciscans, vowed to hold no property at all and to live lives of the greatest simplicity. The Dominicans, originating around the same time, were primarily a teaching order.

Above, a black-robed Dominican friar. Saint Francis (right) is shown kneeling before Pope Honorius III, who gives him a document recording papal approval of the rule of the Franciscan order. Francis had difficulty securing acceptance for his new order because local priests resented competing with peripatetic Franciscan friars for the attention of parishoners. As a result, Franciscans were not allowed to preach theology and were required to confine their efforts to encouraging morality.

CARMELITANI

BENEDETTO NELLE INDIE

71

S. FRANCESCO DI PAOLA

69

HVMILIATI

CAPVCCINI.

67

Above, a Capuchin monk, wearing his characteristic pointed hood. Below, members of various religious orders (left to right): a Carmelite; a Benedictine; Saint Francis of Paola, wearing a somber black robe and hood; a member of the Order of Humiliati, which was suppressed in the sixteenth century because of its ties with heretics; a Carthusian; a member of the Order of Saint John of God; a Cistercian; and an Armenian monk.

CERTOSINI

HOSPITALARII DI GIO DI DIO
NOMINATI I BEN FRATELLI

CISTERCIENSI

MONACI ARMENI

43

troversy about icon worship. So, in what turned out to be a momentous decision, the pope turned his back on the Byzantines and linked his fortunes to the Franks.

Under the protection of Charles and his bodyguards, the pope returned safely to Rome. The alliance between pope and king was not destined to end there. A few decades earlier, Pepin had needed the moral support of the pope; now Leo needed the political protection of a Frankish king. Accordingly, Leo arranged one of the most theatrical scenes in the history of the Church.

On Christmas Day, in the year 800, as Charles knelt in prayer at St. Peter's Basilica, Pope Leo descended from the altar and placed a jeweled crown on the Frank's head. According to a contemporary account, the congregation chanted, three times: "To Charles, the most pious Augustus, crowned of God, the great and peace-giving emperor, be life and victory." Charles avowed to have been unprepared for the honor—a claim that has been vigorously debated. Whatever his true sentiments were, Charles accepted the title of emperor—heir and successor to the empire of the Caesars that had ended 324 years earlier—and used it the rest of his life.

Inherent in the symbolism of a pope anointing an

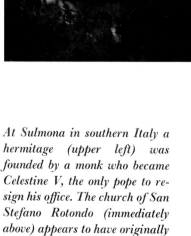

At Sulmona in southern Italy a hermitage (upper left) was founded by a monk who became Celestine V, the only pope to resign his office. The church of San Stefano Rotondo (immediately above) appears to have originally been a market building in imperial Rome. A detail of a painting (right) by Taddeo Gaddi shows Saint Francis' sponsor, Pope Innocent III.

emperor "in God" was a new understanding of the prerogatives of king and pope: Charles now laid claim to spiritual authority and Leo to secular power. In fact, by anointing an emperor, the pope had assumed for himself the highest temporal power—that of king maker. This occasion also officially consecrated the so-called theory of the two swords, which stated that Christ gave the pope authority to use secular as well as spiritual sanction over the *corpus christianum* (the Christian empire and its people). From this moment, church and state were theoretically united in a divine partnership. In reality, the stage was set for the frequent antagonisms that would mar relations between church and state for centuries to come, as both sought to assert competing claims to authority in the West.

For the moment, the alliance proved harmonious. Not long after his coronation at St. Peter's, Charles embarked upon an ambitious campaign to strengthen the Carolingian territories he had inherited and, at the same time, to promote the ideals of a unified Christian state. Charles not only wanted to extend his political influence but also to fulfill his duty as a Christian monarch, so he assumed a leading role in the government of the Church. As "the most pious Augustus, crowned of God," Charlemagne actively

This famous painting (above) by Giotto shows Saint Francis preaching to the birds. An early biography reports that Francis would bless the birds and give them leave to fly away. "My brother birds," he would say, "much ought ye to praise your Creator ... who has given you feathers for clothing, wings for flight, and all that ye have need of. God has made you noble among his creatures." The saint's remains rest in this sarcophagus (right) at Assisi.

supported church reforms and enjoined the clergy to maintain high moral standards:

> Bishops and priests shall live according to the canons [law of the Church] and shall teach others to do the same . . . no bishops, abbots, priests' deacons, or other members of the clergy shall presume to have dogs for hunting, or hawks, falcons, and sparrow hawks . . . the canonical clergy . . . shall be instructed at the episcopal residence or in the monastery with all diligence.

Charlemagne's dream of an imperial church did not survive long after his death. Under his successors, who lacked his extraordinary energy, the empire was weakened by internal dissension and frequent invasions from without. From this disintegration, the Church emerged strengthened, as power passed from the emperors to the popes. In time, however, the fragmentation of the Frankish kingdom exacted a price: The localism that plagued the imperial administration of the empire also infected the Church. Increasingly, bishops found themselves at the mercy of local tyrants, and the popes found it more and more difficult to administer to the needs of their far-flung dioceses or impress the ideals of a unified Christian state.

In 1227, Pope Gregory IX (below left) ex-communicated the Holy Roman emperor Frederick II for failing to fulfill a vow to embark on a crusade to the Holy Land. Neither that excommunication nor a subsequent one proved effective. In response to these moves, Frederick decided to march on Rome, but Gregory died before Frederick attacked. Innocent IV, one of Gregory's successors, called a church council (far left) at Lyon in France to condemn Frederick and declare a crusade against him, but Frederick died before the crusade could begin. Clement IV (above left) continued the struggle against the emperors by inviting the French into Italy to oppose them. The French, however, proved even more difficult to control than the Holy Roman emperors.

Saint Thomas Aquinas (top) was an ardent thirteenth-century supporter of the supremacy of the popes. Right, three of the popes who reigned during the thirteenth century (top to bottom): Honorius IV; his successor, Nicholas IV; and Celestine V, the hermit monk who became pope for a few months and then resigned the papacy.

Pope Boniface VIII (above) instituted the first Holy Year, granting a plenary indulgence to those undertaking a pilgrimage to Rome in 1300. A few years later, as a result of a quarrel with the king of France, Boniface was made a prisoner at Anagni by the king's Italian aides; he died shortly thereafter, in 1303. Near right, the façade of the cathedral of Anagni. Immediately below, the cathedral's interior. Below right, a cloth said to have been worn by Boniface.

In this climate of political turmoil, the authority of the papacy was bolstered by the appearance of the Pseudo-Isidorian decretals, a document probably compiled by a Frankish monk in the ninth century. This spurious document made a claim for the primacy of papal jurisdiction based on both authentic documents and, when needed, convincing forgeries. The so-called Donation of Constantine provided additional support for papal supremacy in matters both spiritual and temporal. This skillful forgery related the story about how Constantine had been cured of leprosy through baptism by Pope Sylvester I. In gratitude, the emperor was said to have transferred his capital to Constantinople so that the bishop of Rome would be free to govern in the West without imperial interference.

These two canons, which were held to be authentic throughout the Middle Ages, established clear precedents for papal supremacy and for freedom from secular interference. Of course, they would have been worthless if the papacy had lacked the authority to enforce them, but they did provide needed theoretical support for the popes who reigned during the dark era that followed the collapse of the Carolingian kingdoms.

By the tenth century, the papacy had its own homeland around Rome, legal jurisdiction over the clergy, and a vast territory over which to exert its jurisdiction. It was during this century, however, that the papacy forfeited much of its influence and prestige. One of its chief weaknesses was corruption from within. As early as the fourth century, Saint Jerome had attacked the indifference and extravagance of the

Constructed under three popes during the fourteenth century, the palace at Avignon covers more than three acres and has walls more than seventeen feet thick. The Italian patriot Cola di Rienzi was kept a prisoner here for attempting to revive the ancient Roman republic and seeking to restore the pope to Rome as a mere bishop.

Innocent VI (left) and Urban V (right) were both determined to restore the papacy to Rome. Urban returned to Rome in 1367, but political complications forced him back to Avignon, where the papacy remained in exile for nearly a decade longer. Innocent was noted for his efforts to reform the Church. He prohibited the holding of more than one church office and attempted to reunify Christendom.

clergy in Rome. Contemporary reports argued that "being made rich ... dressing splendidly, feasting luxuriously ..." were among the rewards of being elected pope. Corruption was common at all levels of the church hierarchy, from incontinent bishops to ignorant clerics.

One ubiquitous corruption was the buying and selling of church offices, a trade that was to become known as simony, from the name of Simon Magnus, who offered Saint Peter money for the gift of the holy spirit. In this corrupt market, bishops and priests received their offices from lords, the appointments going to the highest bidder or to family members.

Secular intervention in church elections inevitably tended to make the clergy more interested in performing the services they owed to their local rulers—acting as heads of estates, secretaries, or judges—than in attending to the spiritual welfare of their parishes.

Lay control over church appointments was not confined to bishops and parish priests. In Rome, the papacy was forced to ally itself with local warlords to suppress civil disorders within the city itself as well as to stave off frequent invaders. Dependence on these local protectors inevitably involved the popes in unsavory political intrigues. As early as the ninth century, Rome's leading families began to treat the office

Boniface IX, who became pope in 1389, was forced to deal with a succession of antipopes, represented here (above) as wolves assaulting the papal throne. Clement VII (left) was the first antipope in the decades-long papal schism, John XXIII (right) the last.

Florence's cathedral (immediately above and above right) was the center of a city where art and learning were prized. When a revolution in 1434 drove Pope Eugene IV from Rome, the pope found refuge in Florence, where he became exposed to Renaissance ideals. Below, Eugene IV's coat of arms. Right, a manuscript illustration showing Eugene consecrating the cathedral at Florence.

The fifteenth century saw numerous attempts to reunify a church torn by dissension. Several councils were summoned to heal the papal schism, but often they only exacerbated the situation. Left, a scene at a fourteenth-century council. Meanwhile, the Church and the papacy continued the struggle against heresy. Above, a Renaissance painting that shows Saint Thomas Aquinas battling heresy.

of the pope as a commodity, something that could be bought or sold or finagled by their most unscrupulous relatives. One family controlled and debased it for generations. The anarchical conditions of the tenth century also damaged the Church outside Italy. In France, it was not uncommon for feudal lords to abuse their control over church offices or churchmen to ignore their spiritual duties.

The Church's detractors have always made much of this disreputable period. But even in the darkest days of the papacy, there were forces of good at work within the Church, movements against corruption and for beneficial administration. Perhaps the most successful, and certainly the most far-reaching, of these reform movements began at the monastery of Cluny in Burgundy in 910. Its founder, William, duke of Aquitaine, was well acquainted with the problem of lay interference in the Church, and he safeguarded his monastery by putting it under the direct control of the papacy. The discipline, morality, and administrative ability that characterized the earliest Cluniac abbots were so exemplary that the Cluniacs were often enlisted to reform other monasteries. Scores of these reformed orders were, in effect, annexed to the congregation of Cluny and became subject to periodic supervisory visitations by traveling Cluniac

abbots. At its height, Cluny was reported to have had hundreds of these affiliates, not only in France but also in England, Germany, Spain, and Italy.

The triumph of the Cluniacs in the sphere of spiritual reform also extended to the arts, particularly architecture. The Cluniacs were great church builders. In fact, the architectural activity that began with the reformed monasteries eventually spread throughout Europe. This architectural awakening both reflected and enhanced the growing influence of the Church. In the words of the famous chronicler Raoul Glaber:

Soon after the year 1000 all over the world, and especially in Italy and France, people began to rebuild their churches. Most of them were well constructed and in no need of alterations, but all Christian countries were rivalling each other to see which should have the most beautiful temples. One would have said that the world was shaking itself and throwing off its old rags, to reclothe itself in a white robe of churches.

The emergence of the reform party at Cluny was paralleled by the rise of a new political organization in Germany. Henry III (1039–1056) was a fervent supporter of the Cluniac reform. He did not hesitate, however, to appoint his own men to important ecclesiastical positions throughout the empire, the

Left, Pope Paul II's coat of arms. Paul encouraged Renaissance scholars and artists to concentrate on religious themes in their work, as Michaelangelo did in his famous ceiling for the Sistine Chapel (above). Scholars and artists proved more interested in classical antiquity, however. Right, the eminent classical scholar Platina being received by Pope Sixtus IV.

fundamental political strategy of German kings for securing order in their kingdom; these appointees were political rulers as well as spiritual leaders, allies to the king but also, theoretically, subservient to the pope. Like his predecessors, Henry also took an active interest in the papacy and virtually appointed his cousin Bruno, a Cluny-inspired reformer, to Peter's chair in 1049. Bruno took the name Leo IX.

With Leo, a great period in papal history begins. The eleventh century marks a period of growth and of deepening papal influence on all aspects of European life. Leo reorganized the cardinalate at Rome. Previously, the role of the cardinals had been largely ceremonial, and the cardinals were usually sinecures of the Roman nobility. The new pope appointed non-Italians to the office, in this way breaking the hold of the Roman nobility on the Curia, and then used his appointees as agents and advisors. Leo himself presided over synods in Germany and France—a conspicuous symbol of papal authority. These church councils condemned simony, reaffirmed clerical celi-

bacy, and insisted that "no one shall be promoted to ecclesiastical rulership without the choice of the clergy and people."

This last declaration of the independence of the Church was a central tenet of the reform party. Henry III died in 1056, and since his heir was only six at the time, a regency ruled in his stead. The reform party in Rome seized this moment to sever the papacy from imperial control. Popes were elected without the advice of the emperor's regents. One reformer, Cardinal Humbert, went so far as to deny the validity of lay appointments to ecclesiastical office and to attack the practice of lay investiture, the customary procedure

for filling episcopal vacancies. During the investiture ceremony, the king would appoint the new bishop by "investing" him with the ring and staff, symbols of his authority. As a result, the bishops owed two allegiances, one to the Church, the other, in their role as feudal lords, to the state.

The Holy Roman emperors would not submit to the abandonment of such a powerful weapon. The bitter controversy that resulted from this conflict of visions was not merely a question of the right of appointments. It was a more serious and fundamental battle over the proper ordering of society. Which power was ascendant in Europe: the popes who crowned the emperors or the emperors who allowed themselves to be crowned?

When Pope Alexander II died in 1073, the Roman citizenry rose up, summoned the last of the great reformers, Hildebrand, to the papal quarters, and demanded his election as pope. Hildebrand became Gregory VII, one of the greatest pontiffs in the history of the Church. Two years after Gregory was anointed pope, Henry IV, now of age, was gaining power in Germany. These two strong-willed men were fated to become protagonists in a long and debilitating struggle known as the Investiture Controversy.

The outlines of the controversy are simple. In 1075, Gregory outlawed lay investiture, and in retaliation

The pope was a statesman, a warrior, a patron of the arts, and an administrator, but his primary role was always spiritual. Left, a pope in prayer before a crucifix, liberating a soul from purgatory. Below left, a pope praying before an image of the risen Christ. All too often, however, the popes neglected their religious duties—and artists and reformers attacked them fiercely for it. Below, an allegorical miniature showing a pope with the feet of a devil. Right, a pope being cast into the jaws of hell.

Henry and his bishops invalidated the pope's election. The next move was Gregory's. In 1076, he excommunicated the emperor. In turn, Henry excommunicated the pope. This ever more bitter situation proved advantageous to Henry's rivals in Germany, who now ordered him to reconcile himself to the pope or forfeit his crown. Henry met this challenge with a brilliant act of diplomatic subtlety. His enemies had invited the pope to Germany. In the middle of the winter, Henry, dressed as a penitent, intercepted the pope at Canossa, where he knelt for three days in the snow outside Gregory's window waiting to do penance. The length of his vigil reflects the intensity of the pope's annoyance. Appearing as a simple Christian seeking forgiveness, Henry had exploited the ambiguity of the papacy's dual identity: As a Catholic priest, Gregory could not deny absolution to a penitent—in this case, his political rival.

This rather ambiguous peace ended the first period of the controversy. What was fundamentally at stake was the proper balancing of the uneasy, but absolutely essential, alliance between sacred and secular powers. Gregory himself outlined his understanding of this relationship in a remarkable document, the *Dictatus Papae* [The Statement of the Pope]. In these brief phrases, the pope summarized the grand vision

The Borgias

Alexander used his office to gain advantage for his children, hoping to make Cesare the ruler of a united Italy and to arrange politically expedient marriages for Lucrezia that would strengthen the Borgia family's power. Cesare, ruthless and brutal, was the perfect instrument for the pope's policy. Named a cardinal at the age of eighteen, he was placed in command of the armies charged with finally subjecting the Papal States to firm Roman control. He sadistically strangled and tortured his enemies and once even knifed a papal official who had run to Alexander for refuge and was cowering in fear under the pope's mantle. Cesare's career did not, however, outlast his father's papacy. When Alexander died in 1503, Cesare lost his armies and, soon, his life. Lucrezia lived longer, ending her days as the duchess of Ferrara, a model of aristocratic virtue—bearing children, patronizing literature, and sponsoring charities.

Pope Alexander dearly loved his children—two sons and a daughter—who were born long before he ascended the papal throne in 1492. The names of two of these offspring, Cesare and Lucrezia Borgia, have gone down in history as synonyms for wickedness. At least in the case of Cesare, the reputation is richly deserved; even the pope himself, it is said, was afraid of his son's violence.

One of the main tasks of Cesare Borgia (above) as general in charge of the papal armies was to subdue strongholds in which local warlords held out against the centralized government of the Papal States. San Leo (left) on the eastern coast of Italy was one of the fortresses that Cesare conquered. Cesare's ambition was reflected in the mottoes he had engraved on his sword: "Either Caesar or nothing" and "The die is cast."

The small duchy of Urbino was governed by a succession of highly cultured rulers, including Francesco Maria della Rovere (above). Urbino was able to maintain its independence even though it was theoretically part of the papal domain. At the castle of Ferrara (below), another major center of Renaissance culture, Lucrezia Borgia spent the last years of her life as a duchess.

The tiny principality of San Marino with its crenelated fortress (above) held out against the attacks of all the condottieri (leaders of mercenary armies) of Renaissance Italy but fell to Cesare Borgia for a short time in 1503. Situated atop a crag overlooking the Adriatic, San Marino managed to remain aloof from the strife that racked the Papal States for centuries.

In honor of the jubilee of 1500, Alexander VI minted a coin (left) with his portrait. By Alexander's time, the papal jubilee brought hordes of pilgrims—and substantial revenues—to Rome. Many pilgrims were disgusted by what they saw of papal luxury and corruption. To garner additional income, Alexander extended the length of the jubilee and sold jubilee indulgences to pilgrims unable to come to Rome. Much of the proceeds went for Cesare Borgia's wars.

The struggle for unity

From its earliest days, the Church had to contend with ideas that controverted its teachings and with opposition to the centralization of ecclesiastical government in Rome. The twelfth century saw a violent crusade against Albigensian heretics in France. In the fourteenth and fifteenth centuries, John Wycliffe and John Huss fought against the papacy in England and Bohemia, the Italian Marsilius of Padua maintained that the Church should own nothing, and the Englishman William of Ockham contested the pope's temporal power. Some religious thinkers went so far as to call the pope the antichrist, but most reformers attempted change within the framework of the Church.

In the seventeenth century, the Dutchman Cornelis Jansen (above) attacked the Church's decline in spirituality.

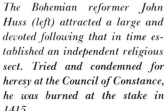

The Bohemian reformer John Huss (left) attracted a large and devoted following that in time established an independent religious sect. Tried and condemned for heresy at the Council of Constance, he was burned at the stake in 1415.

The principle of sun-centered planetary motion enunciated by the great Polish astronomer Nicolaus Copernicus contradicted the traditional view of the universe and was seen as subversive to the Church's teachings. Below, a representation of the Copernican system.

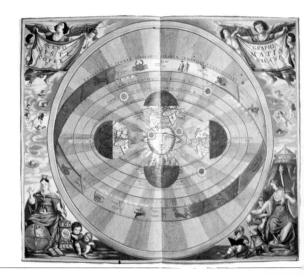

Toward the end of the fifteenth century, a religious revival led by Girolamo Savonarola (above) swept through Florence. In his sermons, Savonarola, a Dominican, vehemently denounced secular corruption and ecclesiastical worldliness. Under his direction, personal ornaments were heaped upon bonfires, Florence's prostitutes were exiled, and the populace spent days in fasting and prayer. Inevitably there was a reaction. Savonarola was imprisoned, tortured until he confessed that he had inspired the revival to glorify himself, hanged, and burned (left).

The Dutch scholar and philosopher Desiderius Erasmus (left) satirized ecclesiastical corruption but refused to abandon the Church as many other reformers did. Europe's most respected intellectual leader, he kept many followers faithful to the papacy.

When the Italian Galileo Galilei (right) wrote a work in support of Copernicus' theory that the earth revolved around the sun, the astronomer was summoned to Rome. There he was forced to promise that he would never write anything to contradict the Church's teachings on the universe. For centuries, Galileo's case was cited as evidence that the papacy would never adapt to the modern world.

of the medieval papacy at the same time that he was involved in a struggle that proved the fragility of the institution:

the pope can be judged by no one;

the Roman church has never erred and never will err till the end of time;

the Roman church was founded by Christ alone;

the pope alone can depose and restore bishops;

he alone can make new laws, set up new bishoprics, and divide old ones;

he alone can translate bishops;

he alone can call general councils and authorize canon law;

he alone can revise his own judgments;

he alone can use the imperial insignia;

he can depose emperors;

he can absolve subjects from their allegiance;

all princes should kiss his feet;

his legates, even though in inferior orders, have precedence over all bishops;

an appeal to the papal court inhibits judgment by all inferior courts;

a duly ordained pope is undoubtedly made a saint by the merits of St. Peter.

The ideal lines of medieval society were thus drawn. At the apex, above all other rulers, stood the pope,

The painter Raphael sketched the designs for the works in the Vatican's "Raphael Loggia" (left). He also designed the frescoes of the Palazzo Farnesina (below), which was built by his patron, the pope's banker.

During the Renaissance, the church of Santa Maria Maggiore (right) was lavishly adorned. Its ceiling is gilded with what reportedly was the first shipment of gold sent back from America. Several popes are buried in the church.

who alone was empowered by God. This claim to supremacy invariably strikes the modern reader as arrogant and foolish, and there are elements of both in Gregory's claim. Yet the *Dictatus* captured the essence of an understanding of sacred authority and a hierarchical world order that dated back to the fourth century.

Nonetheless, Gregory would soon be reminded, as all popes eventually were, of the vulnerability of the papal temporal authority. While the emperor was kneeling in the snows of Canossa, his enemies in Germany elected an antiking, Rudolf of Swabia. Germany then entered on a long and devastating civil war which the pope used to weaken the power of the Holy Roman emperor. At first he supported neither side, hoping thus to prolong the war, though eventually he declared himself in favor of Rudolf—a mistake, as it turned out. (The declaration of temporal authority necessitated such tactics since the Vatican never had an army powerful enough to support its claims.) Rudolf was killed in battle, and in 1084 Henry captured Rome, installed an antipope, and had himself crowned emperor. Gregory's Norman vassals and allies arrived too late to help him, and he died defeated in 1085.

The Investiture Controversy dragged on until

1122, when a compromise settlement was reached in the so-called Concordat of Worms. By mutual agreement, ecclesiastical elections in Germany were to be free and ordered according to canon law (the laws of the Church). The emperor also renounced the practice of investing the new bishops with the symbols of spiritual office, and the pope granted the emperor the right to invest bishops with the symbols of their temporal authority. The papacy was now free to develop its authority.

The twelfth and thirteenth centuries witnessed the intricate and extensive growth of papal government. Legates, the pope's agents, were sent out on the pope's business throughout Europe. Career seekers traveled to Rome to buy the pope's favor, powerful monastic orders sought preferments and special dispensations. Men from all ranks of society were anxious to obtain papal protection and adjudication of their legal problems in the papal court. The papal court also laid down the rules of proper Christian conduct, ordered relations among competing groups, and watched over the lives of the clergy. The Vatican worked in these years as an efficient bureaucracy at the heart of medieval society.

In time, many Christians came to regard the development of the papal bureaucracy with distrust, even horror. The popes increasingly became consumed by the often petty details of managing the papal state. Between the years 1159 and 1303, every important pope was a lawyer. The papal court was choked with cases. As Saint Bernard of Clairvaux wrote in 1153: "What slavery can be more degrading and more unworthy of the Sovereign Pontiff than to be kept thus busily employed, I do not say every day, but every hour of every day, in furthering the sordid designs of greed and ambition? . . . What remains over to thee for instructing the people, for edifying the church. . . ?"

Furthermore, the papacy was still hopelessly dependent on the civil powers of Europe. Innocent III's crusade against heretical groups in southern France in 1208 could only be carried out with the approval of the French monarch. The papacy was powerless to

Ferdinand and Isabella of Spain commissioned the building of a circular chapel (above left) on the site of Saint Peter's crucifixion in Rome. Pope Julius II (left) was a leading patron of art during the Renaissance. Michelangelo worked many years on sculptures for a monumental tomb that Julius planned for himself. "I am thy drudge," the artist wearily wrote to the pope. Michelangelo's famous statue of Moses (right) is often said to be a portrait of Julius.

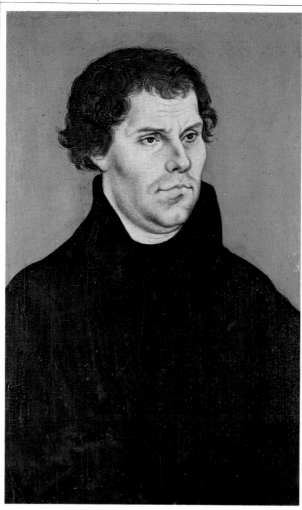

Left, Martin Luther. Above, Luther's wife—Katharina von Bora, a former nun.

The Reformation

Luther taught at the University of Wittenberg in Saxony, where Frederick the Wise sheltered him from opponents' attacks. From the castle of Wittenberg (near right) and his own house (below), Luther was able to disseminate his ideas freely. He is buried in the castle's chapel.

Born the son of a German copper miner in 1483, Martin Luther was to have as profound an effect on Christianity as any pope. A monk whose main interest originally lay in reforming himself ("I am dust and ashes and full of sin," he once wrote), he eventually directed his prodigious mind and bountiful energy toward a reform of the entire Church. Outraged by the selling of indulgences to raise money for the building of St. Peter's Basilica and by the assurance that believers could purchase God's forgiveness for future sins, Luther rebelled against the papacy, won support from German princes and the German people, and set about changing the Church. He rejected several basic doctrines, reduced the number of sacraments, and declared it proper for clergymen to marry. His break with the Church marked the birth of Protestantism.

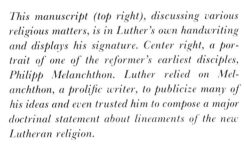

This manuscript (top right), discussing various religious matters, is in Luther's own handwriting and displays his signature. Center right, a portrait of one of the reformer's earliest disciples, Philipp Melanchthon. Luther relied on Melanchthon, a prolific writer, to publicize many of his ideas and even trusted him to compose a major doctrinal statement about lineaments of the new Lutheran religion.

The eminent German theologian Johann Eck (left) engaged Luther in a debate at the University of Leipzig. In the course of the argumentation, Eck forced Luther to admit that he was rejecting papal authority. The Frenchman John Calvin (right) embraced the Reformation and founded a theocratic government in Geneva that became a focal point for the defense of Protestantism.

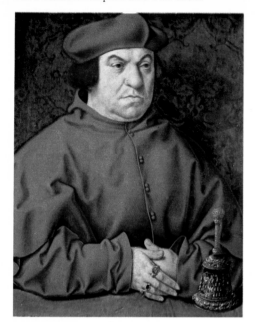

Pope at the time that Luther issued his defiant challenge to papal power, Leo X (near right) was unable to deal with the problem effectively. At the pope's left in this Raphael portrait is Cardinal Giulio de' Medici, who became Clement VII in 1523. Facing page, below, a papal ducat of Clement VII. Far right, Clement's troops attacking one of the gates of Siena in 1526. Bernhard von Cles (above), bishop and prince of the city of Trent, was a firm opponent of the Reformation and an adviser to Holy Roman Emperor Charles V in the early sixteenth century.

resolve in its favor the terrible political struggles in Germany that destroyed the office of the Holy Roman emperor and left the papacy vulnerable to the pretensions of the increasingly powerful French monarchy.

There were other, less obvious, reasons for the gradual decline of papal power in the later Middle Ages. The rise of universities throughout Europe bred a new class of secular intellectuals who were anxious to justify the claims of nationalizing princes against Rome. The law school at Bologna claimed civil law as its own discipline, ignoring even the papal claim to the authority of granting degrees. In England and France, the more far-sighted political leaders were moving to dominate the ecclesiastic structures of their kingdoms. At the same time, political science and legal science became nationalist weapons against the

papacy, and they were wielded convincingly by members of the rising and impatient middle class.

Catholic culture of the Middle Ages achieved its deepest maturity by the middle of the thirteenth century. Thomas Aquinas, a Dominican theologian (1225–1274), gave voice to this moment. Aquinas taught that civil society was necessary and natural, not the result of sin as earlier church theologians had maintained. It was possible for him to argue, therefore, that the "spiritual and the secular power are both derived from the divine power; and therefore the secular power is under the spiritual only in so far as it has been subjected to it by God: namely in those things that pertain to the salvation of the soul."

His argument diverges radically from the claims of Gregory the Great and Gregory VII for the supremacy of the Church. Aquinas continues: "In those

things that pertain to the civil good, the secular power is to be obeyed rather than the spiritual." Here, Aquinas reveals how far the differentiation of church and state had proceeded in theory by this time. But then he concludes, "Useless, perhaps, the secular power is joined to the spiritual, as in the pope, who holds the apex of both authorities, the spiritual and the secular." The papacy would cling stubbornly to this vision well into the nineteenth century.

Other individuals had different ideas. The influence of the Capetian dynasty in France had been deepening throughout the long and costly struggles between the papacy and the Holy Roman emperors. One of the most powerful, ambitious, and unscrupulous of the Capetians, Philip the Fair, came to the throne in 1285. Philip was intent on consolidating royal power, and to this end, he violated the rights of

Castel Sant'Angelo

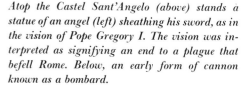

Atop the Castel Sant'Angelo (above) stands a statue of an angel (left) sheathing his sword, as in the vision of Pope Gregory I. The vision was interpreted as signifying an end to a plague that befell Rome. Below, an early form of cannon known as a bombard.

Originally built as a tomb by the emperor Hadrian and used as a mausoleum by succeeding Roman emperors, Castel Sant'Angelo served as the pope's chief fortress for centuries. Named for the angel that Pope Gregory I saw while praying at the site for an end to a plague in Rome, this castle overlooking the Tiber sheltered the popes throughout the Middle Ages when they were threatened by invading armies or by rebellious Roman mobs. Here Pope Clement VII sat mournful and powerless while Rome was sacked in 1527.

In addition to papal apartments, Castel Sant'Angelo contains dungeons in which prisoners, among them the goldsmith and sculptor Benvenuto Cellini, were formerly incarcerated. It also has a hall used for theatrical performances and an armorer's workshop, where weapons for the papal armies were at one time manufactured.

"Why hast thou brought me forth out of the womb?" Clement VII (left) reproached God during the sack of Rome, when the pope was imprisoned in Castel Sant'Angelo. After Clement's papacy, rooms in the castle became increasingly luxurious. Right, the library. Immediately below, the Perseus Room and its papal chair.

In Castel Sant'Angelo's Secret Archives Room (below left), large wooden chests were used to store papal treasures and vestments. Around the wall were cupboards containing the archives of the popes. The castle, strong enough to resist any siege, was rarely used as a papal residence after the sixteenth century.

"Men like Benvenuto" Pope Paul III said, "stand above the law." Benvenuto Cellini (below) was one of the great artists of the Renaissance, and popes gladly winked at his scandalous private life to have him work for them. Cellini claimed to have defended the papacy on the ramparts of Castel Sant'Angelo during the 1527 siege of Rome.

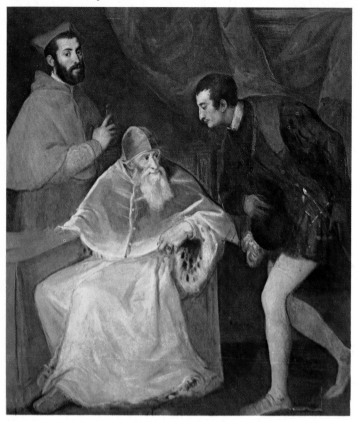

Pope Paul III (above) convened the Council of Trent (facing page, above) in the mid-sixteenth century to help bring about needed Church reforms.

Facing page, below, a sixteenth-century vision of hell.

Below, a view of the Vatican caves.

all the estates of the realm, particularly those of the Church. In his seemingly inexhaustible need for money to fund his centralizing efforts, Philip placed heavy taxes on ecclesiastical property.

The French king Philip found himself confronted with a very powerful adversary, however, in Boniface VIII; who in 1294 was elected to the chair of Peter. Two years later, Boniface forbade taxation of church property in the bull *Clericis Laicos.* Rulers impose heavy burdens on priests and monks, Boniface wrote, and tax them beyond reason. Their purpose in this is not merely financial, though, because these rulers "try to bring [the clergy] into slavery and subject them to their authority." The real fear of the papacy was that the independence of the Church, and thus the integrity of the word of God, would be enslaved to the dreams of princes.

In retaliation, Philip placed an embargo on the export from France of precious metals, jewelry, and currency. This proved so damaging to papal and Italian finance that Boniface was compelled to retreat. The pope decreed that in an emergency, such as the war with England, the French king had the privilege of taxing the Church. He also left it to the king to decide what constituted an emergency.

The second phase of the contest began when Philip arrested Bernard Saisset, papal ambassador to the French court, on charges of treason. Saisset was tried by a French court, convicted, and imprisoned, in direct violation of canon law which stated that only the pope could try a bishop. Boniface replied with a bull entitled *Ausculta Fili* [Listen, Son], reminding Philip that "God has set us over kings and kingdoms." He demanded that Saisset be released immediately and peremptorily summoned Philip and his bishops to Rome to attend a council on the state of the Church in France.

The king's next move revealed how novel a situation Boniface was confronting. The king called the first meeting of the Estates-General, which would later become the French parliament, in April of 1302. Clergy, nobles, and commoners met in Notre Dame where they were told by Philip's minister, Pierre Flotte, that France had an integrity derived from God alone and that the pope had no power within its boundaries. The meeting approved Philip's resistance, to the great embarrassment of the French clergy but with their silent acquiescence.

In rebuttal Boniface penned the strongest affirmation of the temporal sovereignty ever to emerge from Rome, the bull *Unam Sanctam* (November 1302). Against Philip's national pretensions, Boniface proclaimed "there is one holy, Catholic and apostolic church . . . and outside this church there is no salva-

tion or remission of sins." The pope met the challenge of Philip's centralization of royal power with the statement, "the spiritual power has to institute the earthly power and to judge it if it has not been good."

By this time Philip had wearied of words. He sent agents to Italy to kidnap Boniface. They met the pope on September 7, 1303, in the northern Italian town of Anagni, where legend has it that one of them slapped Boniface across the face. Whether or not the "slap of Anagni" was real or merely symbolic is not known,

The saintly Pius V (right) was originally a Dominican monk. Although surrounded by the luxury of the Vatican, Pius strictly adhered to rigid monastic discipline throughout his papacy.

Below, a miniature from a sixteenth-century manuscript, with a symbolic representation of Pope Gregory XIII, a notable reformer.

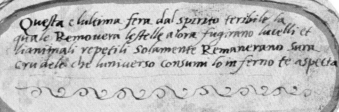

but the papacy was humiliated. Boniface, over eighty at the time and suffering badly from "the stone," died a month later.

Boniface was succeeded first by the short-lived Benedict XI (1303–1304) and then Pope Clement V (1305–1314), who was a mere pawn in the hands of the French king. Not only did he exonerate Philip of any guilt in the attack on Boniface, but he modified the *Unam Sanctam* to such a degree that the revision constituted a practical revocation. The degradation of the papacy was completed in 1309 with the removal of the papal seat to Avignon, where it remained until 1377.

Anarchy soon overtook Rome, and a chorus of sincere Christians, including Petrarch and Saint Catherine of Siena, implored the restoration of the papacy to Italy. This, and the necessity of preserving papal

interests in the damaged city, induced Gregory XI (1370–1378) to return to Rome in 1377. The Roman people greeted him with solemnity and relief, but he was to die within a year. The Roman populace had no intention, however, of losing the pope again. Under popular pressure, the cardinals chose an Italian, Bartolommeo Prignano, as Urban VI (1378–1389). Urban quickly offended the French by his tactless efforts at reinstituting Italian authority. The same group of cardinals met again four months later

In 1582, Gregory XIII introduced a more accurate calendar to replace the Julian calendar, which had been in use since ancient times. Below, Gregory at a lecture to explain the reform.

An eighteenth-century procession with the pope and his court (right) travels across the Tiber toward St. Peter's, which can be seen in the background. There were frequent occasions for the pope to cross from the right bank of the Tiber, where St. Peter's and the Vatican are located, to the left bank, where most Romans lived.

Above, a view of a seventeenth-century consistory.

Left, the pope's Swiss guards at a festival. This depiction (above right) of a game of boccie being played in Rome is from a sixteenth-century Dutch painting. Near right, crowds being contained outside the Palazzo Barberini during a party.

and elected Robert of Geneva as Clement VII (1378–1394), who moved his court back to Avignon.

The scandal of the papal schism shocked Western Christendom. Two popes, both properly elected, claimed the title of Vicar of Christ. This was a most devastating rivalry. It was still the belief of the age that the papacy was the foundation of European culture; now that assurance was shattered. It was against this background that conciliar theory emerged as an alternative to papal authority. Conciliarists maintained that there was an authority in the Church, located either in the people or in political rulers, independent and superior to papal authority. This au-

thority was to be expressed in representative, ecumenical councils organized by nation. The pope was bound to obey the council, since it represented in an immediate way the entire Church.

Though conciliarism was offered by many as a sincere program of reform, it soon became a weapon in the hands of national leaders. Aggrandizing rulers used it to authorize their domination of the Church within their territories. Canon lawyers maintained that in an emergency, the Holy Roman emperor could summon a council, in this way giving the emperor a way of pressuring and coercing reluctant popes into cooperation.

Despite these dangers, it was a general council, meeting in Constance in November 1414, which ended the schism. The council was summoned in a joint decree prepared by Pope John XXIII and the Holy Roman emperor Sigismund. The conciliar delegates deposed all claimants to the chair of Peter. When one of the popes attempted to subvert the meeting, an official statement was prepared declaring that the council "representing the Catholic Church militant, has its power immediately from Christ, and everyone . . . is bound to obey it. . . ." In 1417, the council elected Pope Martin V (1417–1431). The business of the council was concluded with the de-

mand of the delegates that Martin call another assembly in five years.

The papacy was, naturally, displeased by this undisguised usurpation of its authority, and early in his pontificate, Martin prohibited all further appeals to a council for adjudication of religious affairs. From Constance to the Council of Trent, which met during the Reformation, the papacy set itself firmly against every popular call for a reform council as a precaution against the erosion of the authority of Rome and the pope.

The attack on papal authority in Italy during the Avignon period and the continuing powerlessness of

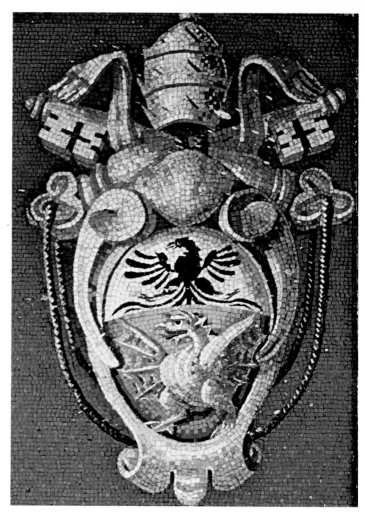

Near left, the coat of arms of Paul V (Camillo Borghese), one of the great builders of papal Rome. Paul completed the beautiful Borghese palace (below left), which stands high on one of Rome's seven hills. A close relative of the pope was responsible for the restoration of the church of San Gregorio Magno (far left).

the Holy Roman emperor, coincident with the rise in power and wealth of the northern Italian city-states, were key developments in the era of intense creativity known as the Renaissance. Critical thinking, linguistic studies, and close study of the Gospels all characterized this moment in European history, a moment that posed a threat to the papacy. The precise nature of this danger was revealed around the year 1440 when the humanist Lorenzo Valla exposed the falsity of the Donation of Constantine. But there was also great promise. The Renaissance witnessed the appearance of new forms of piety, a new scholarly interest in the church fathers, and a renewed devotion to the New Testament.

The popes, restored to Rome, found that the Church had become the object of the political ambitions of the Roman nobility. Almost immediately the papacy descended into the maelstrom of Italian politics in an effort to recapture its diminished authority on the peninsula. This proved a bitter and unscrupulous quest. Sixtus IV (1471–1484), for example,

The brief reign of Leo XI (top left), a member of the Medici family of Florence, preceded Paul V's accession to the papacy in 1605. Paul was notable as a patron of the arts and of buildings. Above, Paul presiding over a meeting of ambassadors, cardinals, and various Church officials.

warred to advance the interests of his family, as did the Borgia pope, Alexander VI (1492–1503). The latter used his authority mainly to increase the power of his infamous son, Cesare Borgia. Alexander was succeeded by Julius II, the warrior pope, who led his own armies into battle to protect the Papal States. (The humanist Erasmus of Rotterdam wrote a bitter satire against Julius in which he depicted the pope trying to bully his way into Paradise.) Leo X (1513–1521), a Medici and the worldliest of the Renaissance popes, followed Julius.

The Renaissance popes were aristocratic and cultured men, almost all of them capable, some of them

immoral. Several of them had reputations as humanist scholars and poets. They used the wealth of the Vatican to commission magnificent works of art. The popes patronized Botticelli, Leonardo da Vinci, and Titian, among many others, summoning them to Rome to create a city ever more commensurate with papal power and prestige. Julius commissioned Michelangelo to paint the ceiling of the Sistine Chapel and instituted work on St. Peter's Basilica. Yet many of them also attempted to heed the cries of reform that reached Rome from every corner of Christendom. Paul II condemned simoniacal practices, was scrupulous in the appointment of bishops and advisors, and maintained a strict discipline at the papal court. Julius convoked the Fifth Lateran Council in Rome in 1512, in part to counterbalance an antipapal conference being held at the same time under the sponsorship of the French king, but also to raise the issue of reform.

None of these reform efforts, however, was very successful. Besieged by the aggressive tactics of Francis I of France, England's Henry VIII, and even the devout Catholics Ferdinand and Isabella, the popes were afraid to initiate any reforms of the papacy itself. Such political considerations made them wary of reform, which they took to be an attack on their authority.

Absorbed by Italian dynastic intrigues and the press of legal affairs, the papacy gradually lost touch with the needs of the Church. The expanded European economy nurtured a new urban class of men and women who looked for protection not to Rome or to the episcopal sees that had governed Europe in the Middle Ages but to their national princes, who in

turn were augmenting their power at the expense of the Church. Ecclesiastical taxation, long a burden, was now resented as an intrusion into national life. The voice of this anxiety was amplified by the discovery of the printing press. Among the words the people wanted to see for themselves were those of the Gospel, and if they could not get these through approved channels they would go underground to ob-

The exuberant life of papal Rome is evident in this view of the Corso, Rome's main street (above left), with its heavy carriage and pedestrian traffic. Many of the passers-by are clerics, as can be seen from the broad-brimmed hats. Left, a rediscovered ancient statue that came to be called Madama Lucrezia.

The Piazza Navona (above), surrounded with churches and palaces, was a stadium in ancient Roman times. Fountains were added in the seventeenth century. This 1634 painting shows the piazza being used for a tournament.

The Feathered Serpent and The Cross

tain them. At the heart of this unrest lurked the over-riding question of the sixteenth century: How can I be saved? The papacy could no longer offer a meaningful or convincing answer.

Anxiety over personal salvation and emergent nationalism came together in the person of the German monk Martin Luther. The immediate issue was Luther's outrage over the increased sale of indulgences (the remission of time spent in Purgatory through good works or financial donations) in Germany. Salvation, Luther preached, was not a reward for good works or a prize for manipulating the great Catholic machine of indulgences, devotions, pen-

In the mid-seventeenth century, Pope Alexander VII (bottom) encountered difficulties with Portugal and France, both of which sought to counter papal influence in their national churches. But Alexander scored a triumph when Queen Christina of Sweden (below left) abdicated, converted to Catholicism, and moved to Rome. Below, a pageant in honor of the queen, with 280 performers presenting a mock battle between "Amazons" and "Cavaliers." Christina observed the spectacle from a box in the Palazzo Barberini, seen at the right of this painting.

ances, and sacraments. Rather it was to believe in Christ's saving act despite the painful and incontrovertible evidence of human sin. This understanding is revealed, Luther taught, not in the papal bulls, but in Scripture.

Luther's ideas were not clearly developed when Luther nailed his Ninety-Five Theses to the door of his church in the small German town of Wittenberg. As Luther followed out the logic of his insight, however, and as the political implications of his thinking became apparent, events swept him forward. In 1518, Leo summoned Luther to Rome. Luther's protector, Elector Frederick of Saxony, managed to have the location switched to the German town of Augsburg, where Luther was ordered by the papal theologian Cajetan to retract. Luther fled Augsburg, and once safely back in Wittenberg, he called for a general council to hear his case. A year later, Luther denied authority even to a general council, allowing appeal only to Scripture. This was blasphemous anarchy in the eyes of his Roman opponents. In 1520, the papal bull of condemnation was issued. In a supreme act of defiance, Luther burned it in the public square of Wittenberg.

In 1521, Leo found himself with an unexpected ally in the burgeoning crisis. Henry VIII of England

Crowds attending a religious ceremony during the papacy of Alexander VII are dwarfed by the vast dome of St. Peter's Basilica (above). Below, a coin struck in the year 1675, during the reign of Clement X, depicting the traditional opening of the Holy Door that marks the beginning of the papal jubilee. Originally the papal jubilee was celebrated every century, but eventually the interval was changed to every twenty-five years.

banned Luther's works and published his own refutation of the reformer, *Assertion of the Seven Sacraments.* Leo rewarded him with the title "Defender of the Faith." This alliance was to prove short-lived, however. In the late 1520s, Henry sought unsuccessfully to have his marriage with Catherine of Aragon annulled. Clement VII (1523–1534) might have granted the annulment were it not for the opposition of the Holy Roman emperor Charles V. Charles was Catherine's nephew, and familial loyalty—as well as the desire to keep Henry occupied and out of trouble—determined the emperor's policy.

Henry then turned to the strong national consciousness and antipapism of England. In 1531, he coerced a declaration out of the convocation of English clergy: He was henceforth to be recognized as the "single and Supreme Lord, and, as far as the Law of Christ allows, even supreme head" of the Church in England. This was followed in 1532 with an act forbidding payment of taxes to Rome. In 1534, Parliament passed the Act of Supremacy, decreeing Henry and his successors supreme rulers of the English church. This act constituted reformation by law, with the full cooperation of Parliament. Though the motives of Parliament were predominantly financial and nationalistic, there was evidence of an undercurrent of Protestant religious sentiment which would deepen in England throughout the sixteenth and seventeenth centuries.

Christendom, for centuries only a most tenuous reality, was dissolving into separate religious and political units. The grand vision of the Middle Ages, which placed the pope at the head of a unified Christian culture, was obscured. The question was, could Catholicism survive the dissolution of Christendom?

In 1519, the Hapsburg Charles V became Holy Roman emperor. At first this seemed to offer hope to the papacy. A devout Catholic, he was sovereign over Spain, the Low Countries, Germany, and most of Italy, a most powerful position from which to reunite Europe. Instead, Charles trapped the papacy in his bloody conflict with Francis I and the House of Valois. When the popes failed to cooperate with his ambitions, the Holy Roman emperor showed no mercy. In May 1527, the emperor's troops sacked Rome and left it in ruins.

At any cost, the papacy now wanted to avoid domination by Charles. Therefore, instead of concentrating on the religious revolt in Germany or on the much-needed reform of the Church, Clement VII and Paul III structured their foreign policy around two objectives: breaking the Hapsburg hold on northern Italy and avoiding a reform council, which they

The church of St. John in the Lateran (right and below), one of Rome's oldest, was built on the site of a palace originally belonging to the rich Laterani family of Rome. The palace was presented to Pope Sylvester I by the emperor Constantine himself. The present interior, with its long rows of imposing columns, dates from the sixteenth century. The impressive façade of the great church was added in the year 1734.

During the eighteenth century the marshy countryside near Rome was often invaded by pirates, whose raids brought them almost to the gates of Rome. Many of the pirates came from the Barbary Coast of North Africa. This eighteenth-century painting (below) shows the capture of a group of pirates near Rome.

Life in papal Rome

"The pope's government is a pure despotism," the French writer Stendhal declared early in the nineteenth century, accusing the pope of ruling Romans with the threat of "the gallows in this world and hell in the next." Most Romans would have disagreed with this assessment. They felt that they lived life to its fullest at the very center of the world, in a city that every civilized person visited at least once in his lifetime. Statesmen, religious leaders, pilgrims, writers, and artists all came to Rome to, as Goethe said, "live among a sensual people" and to see impressive church ceremonies and churches. Although filled with beggars, pickpockets, poverty, and disease, the city had numerous festivals, entertainments, and sights to dazzle the visitor.

The lottery (above) was one of the favorite amusements of Rome's citizens. Some Romans attending public executions counted the number of drops of blood that came from decapitated criminals' heads to bet that number on the lottery. The pope's Swiss guards (below right) carried halberds and wore Renaissance costumes designed by Michaelangelo and Raphael. Below left, members of the papal military forces.

Romans celebrated the days before Lent with pageants, horse races, foot races, and sometimes even bull fights. Above, a horse race on the Corso.

The wastelands outside Rome teemed with highwaymen. Below, two nineteenth-century brigands ogling a young girl.

Above, a papal senator. Papal officials were drawn largely from the Roman aristocracy and were always priests. If a layman wished to appear before a court in the Papal States, he had to don clerical garments.

Left, Pope Clement XII and one of his cardinals. Clement made great efforts to reunite the Eastern and Western churches and founded a seminary whose graduates would labor to that end. He reigned from 1730 to 1740, a time when Europe's intellectual leaders regarded the papacy and religion as insignificant. In response to the growing influence of the Freemasons, whose beliefs and observances the Church considered pagan, Clement issued a bull condemning the fraternity.

feared would further undermine papal authority. But the scandal of a divided Christendom and the efforts of sincere reformers finally secured the convocation of a reform council in the city of Trent. After many delays, the council began its deliberations on December 15, 1545, twenty-six years after Luther's protest.

The Council of Trent marks the beginning of the modern papacy. In accord with papal wishes, the council legislated a new and more carefully enforced obedience to Rome, restructuring Church organization so that papal authority would be known directly on all levels. It also emphasized the necessity of teaching the laity the fundamentals of the faith. A

better-instructed laity, however, demanded a better-educated clergy. What was clearly needed was a clergy trained to meet the attacks of Protestantism with orthodox doctrine and to ensure the faithfulness of the laity. Accordingly, the council ordered the foundation of seminaries throughout Europe, assigning special funds to finance the work. The council also insisted on the central importance of the priest's duties in the parish, thereby hoping to revive the Church on a popular level. Every nation, and particularly every city, would soon be filled with Catholic groups and religious orders dedicated to charitable work, social improvement, and religious education.

The strong centralized papacy of the Tridentine Church represented the triumph of a universal Catholicism against the proponents of national churches. There would be no French Catholicism or Spanish Catholicism—only a reformed *Roman* Catholicism. This affirmation filled the papacy with new life, a vigor that was soon channeled into the foreign missions. In 1622, the Congregation for the Propagation of the Faith was founded to ensure papal authority over the churches in South America. The challenge to papal authority in the West was thus met, in part, by the extension of that authority into a new world.

The Piazza Colonna (top), dominated by an ancient column surmounted by a statue of Saint Paul, was one of the busiest squares of papal Rome. Surrounded by palaces, as so many of Rome's squares were, it was always busy with horsemen and pedestrians. The Quirinal Palace (center) was one of the most important in Rome. Originally a summer residence for the popes, it was later used as a palace by the kings of Italy and is now the official residence of the president of Italy in Rome. Above, Pius VI, the pope at the time of the French Revolution.

Napoleon and the pope

In 1804, Napoleon convinced Pius VII to come to Paris to crown him emperor. The pope and the future emperor met at Fontainebleau (above) outside Paris. Just before the ceremony, however, Pius balked, refusing to take part because Napoleon and his wife, Josephine, had not been married in a religious ceremony. Cardinal Fesch, Napoleon's uncle, therefore presided at a marriage ceremony for Napoleon and Josephine the evening before the coronation.

In order to become emperor, Napoleon, like so many others before him, needed the pope's help. In return for Pius VII's pledge to crown him emperor in 1804, Napoleon agreed to restore to the Church many of the rights which the French Revolution had abrogated. In time, though, he began making unacceptable demands on the pope, insisting, for example, that the pontiff join in hostilities against Napoleonic France's greatest enemy, Britain. The pope's refusals led Napoleon to occupy the Papal States and to issue a decree revoking, as he said, "the Donation of Charlemagne, our august predecessor." When, in response, the pope excommunicated Napoleon, the emperor arrested the pope and carried him off as a prisoner, confining him for years in the northern Italian town of Savona.

Napoleon annexed Rome to the French Empire and attempted to use the entire Church for his own ambitious ends. The sick and elderly Pius VII resisted Napoleon's threats, however, until Napoleon met his downfall. In 1815, Rome was formally restored to the pope.

Left, representatives of France and the papacy signing a treaty in 1801 to end more than a decade of strife between France and the Vatican. French revolutionaries were so contemptuous of the Church that they overthrew the rule of the papacy in Rome in 1798 and melted down three papal tiaras for gold. The Concordat of 1801, inspired by Napoleon, restored peace but did not return Church property.

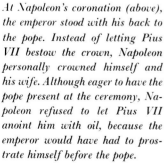

At Napoleon's coronation (above), the emperor stood with his back to the pope. Instead of letting Pius VII bestow the crown, Napoleon personally crowned himself and his wife. Although eager to have the pope present at the ceremony, Napoleon refused to let Pius VII anoint him with oil, because the emperor would have had to prostrate himself before the pope.

Right, top to bottom: Pius VII freeing a cardinal who had been arrested by the French; the pope excommunicating Napoleon; the pope being arrested by French troops; a council of French bishops meeting in 1811 under the watchful eyes of Napoleon's soldiers. "May God pardon him," Pius said about Napoleon, "since for my part I have already pardoned him." Years later, Pius charitably wrote to the allies keeping Napoleon prisoner on Saint Helena, urging them to treat him well.

The strong nationalist sympathies of the Reformation and the chaos of the religious wars that followed it prepared the way for the rise of absolutist monarchies in the seventeenth and eighteenth centuries. Rulers like Louis XIV (1643–1715) of France and Emperor Joseph (1765–1790) of Austria could tolerate no authority in their realms but their own; they therefore sought to bend their national churches to their will. In 1682, the French clergy—at Louis' insistence—sought to diminish papal power by declaring the king superior to the pope in temporal matters and general councils superior in church affairs.

The papacy protested such infringements, but since its own authority, both spiritual and temporal, was absolutist in nature, it was forced into alliance with the great Catholic powers of Europe. When economic, social, and intellectual forces began to undermine Absolutism, the papacy set itself in opposition to the new republicanism. The ultimate clash came in France in 1789, when the French Revolution swept over the Church, reducing its status to that of a civil institution and sending its best representatives into exile.

The French Revolution made its way to Rome in 1798 when French troops occupied the city and established a republican government. Greed was par-

"The people alone are sovereign," reads the inscription at the base of this liberty pole (above), erected to honor the establishment of the Roman Republic of 1798. A liberty cap is seen atop the pole, and a Roman eagle and the words "Roman Republic" are visible below. The soldier leaning on the cannon wears a revolutionary's cockade on his three-cornered hat.

After the French Revolution, the Papal States gradually began to modernize. Pope Gregory XVI, who reigned from 1831 to 1846, opened a new wharf beside the Tiber (below) where steamboats could tie up, thus greatly speeding communication to and from Rome. The popes were long reluctant to allow railroads to approach Rome, however. The city had to wait until the pontificate of Gregory's successor, Pius IX, before a railroad could be built.

In describing one of the towns of the former Papal States, a late nineteenth-century guidebook to Italy remarks: "Sonnino was formerly noted for the picturesque costume of its women and for the audacity of its brigands." Many towns in Italy harbored brigands, who were a great menace to the Papal States. Left, a brigand, wearing a high hat and the laced boots typical of the Roman peasant costume and holding a rifle. Immediately below, a battle between a force of brigands and a troop of mounted papal dragoons in the hills outside Rome. Bottom, convicts in striped clothing marching along a Roman street, headed for forced labor. Behind them walk papal guards.

tially responsible for this attack, particularly a desire for church lands in France and Italy, but it was also the power of Tridentine Catholicism that brought the French to Rome. Catholicism was still a living force among the French masses, a force hostile to the Revolution. The effort to control or destroy Rome was therefore an attack, symbolic and psychological as well as political, at the heart of an opposing vision. The Revolution, according to the radicals, initiated a new history, and the remnants of the old had to be purged. The people of Rome did not welcome the French, but the rioting of the Roman poor for bread in 1795 is an indication that they were ready for a change.

The papacy was traumatized by the Revolution and by the aggressions of Napoleon, both as the leader of the revolutionary army and as pretender to universal authority. Pius VI (1775–1779) was kidnaped by the French and dragged off to France, where he died in exile. Pius VI's successor Pius VII (1800–1823) immediately began the long resistance to revolutionary forces that was to characterize the papacy throughout the nineteenth century.

The tragedy of the papacy in the 1800s stemmed from its inability to remain aloof from "the wars which desolate Europe," as Pius VII told Napoleon.

Chained to the world by the doctrine of the temporal sovereignty, Rome clung obstinately to the Papal States, and when these were taken, the papacy literally imprisoned itself first in Rome and later in the Vatican. In pursuit of this objective, Rome supported the powers of reaction in France and Austria. This alliance was sealed when the reactionary Congress of Vienna returned Rome to Pius VII after Napoleon's defeat.

In 1801, Napoleon, then ascendant in France, signed a concordat with Pius VII, making the French church a virtual department of state under his control. This was only the beginning of the humiliations suffered by Pius. On December 2, 1804, Napoleon summoned the pope to Paris to crown him Holy Roman emperor. Just as Pius was preparing to place the crown on the emperor's head, Napoleon wrested it from the pope and crowned himself, saying "God has given it to me, and woe betide him who takes it away." Napoleon was determined to show the world that his powers rested on no other authority than his own—the pope was but an honorific but dispensable distraction. In 1808, Napoleon invaded Rome and took Pius prisoner. The following year he annexed the Papal States to France and began moving the entire Vatican library to Paris, for Napoleon had visions of

In exile from Rome, Pius IX sails into the tiny harbor of Portici, south of Naples (facing page). Pius was at first eager to reform the government of the Papal States but later developed into a rigid conservative.

Pius IX (below) allowed the first railroads to be built in the Papal States long after a number of countries already had well-developed systems. His predecessors were suspicious of such modern developments. Left, Pius' personal railroad car. Above, Pius preaching in the ancient Roman Forum.

Pius IX attempted to satisfy demands for reform by allowing laymen to take part in papal government. In 1848 one of Pius' lay prime ministers, Pellegrino Rossi, was assassinated (left). Below, the proclamation of the Roman Republic that same year.

The Roman Republic

When revolution broke out in the Papal States in 1848, Pius IX was forced to flee Rome. It was thought that the proclamation of a Roman Republic would lead to the unification of Italy, but France and Austria, the two powers with the greatest interest in Italian affairs, were determined not to let that happen. When Pius appealed to the powers for help, a French army landed in Italy and proceeded to Rome. The republican government had both to quell disturbances inside Rome and to resist a siege by the French outside the city. Elsewhere, Austrian forces were suppressing rebellions in Venice and Tuscany. The goal of Italian political unification was not yet attainable.

Above, smoke from rifle and cannon fire clouding the Roman sky as French troops attack the defenders of the Roman Republic. This encounter took place on the slopes of the Janiculum—one of Rome's seven hills—about a quarter of a mile from St. Peter's Basilica.

Anticipating attack from the French, the republican army prepared a number of fortified positions around Rome. At one of the bastions (left) manned by Italian volunteers, saber-wielding French soldiers lunged at the defenders. Louis Napoleon, who had just become president of France, made the maintenance of papal power in Rome one of the cornerstones of his government's foreign policy.

The 1848 Roman Republic was ruled by a committee of three men. Above, the members of the triumvirate (top to bottom): Carlo Armellini, Giuseppe Mazzini, and Aurelio Saffi. Of the three, Mazzini was by far the most notable. Imprisoned for revolutionary activities, he formed the idea of organizing a group called Young Italy, which sought to unify the country as a republic, non-violently if possible but violently if necessary. The defense forces of the Roman Republic were commanded by Giuseppe Garibaldi. Left, Garibaldi's troops defeating the French at the gate of San Pancrazio on the Janiculum. With Mazzini, Garibaldi is considered one of modern Italy's founding fathers.

controlling not only the present but the past as well.

After Napoleon's defeat and after the Congress of Vienna, the papacy was firmly on the side of reaction. Pius' secretary of state, Cardinal Consalvi, wanted to see a Europe governed by absolute monarchs who would be obedient to the pope in matters concerning the Church. Even under the mildly liberal Pope Pius VII (1800–1823), Consalvi conspired with Metternich to suppress a popular uprising that threatened to violate order in Rome.

Throughout the nineteenth century, the papacy had to rely on French troops for protection. As a result, the popes were compelled to support the restored monarchy and later the government of Louis Napoleon, though this further alienated them from the currents of reform. But the papacy was far from a genuine political power in this period. The popes were incapable of controlling the city of Rome, which remained a city of destitution and suffering, let alone the destiny of Europe.

The end came during the pontificate of Pius IX (1846–1878), one of the longest and most tormented reigns in the Church's history. The single purpose of his papacy was to preserve the political independence of the Church and to prevent it from becoming doctrinally contaminated by the currents of intellectual liberalism. In 1864, the pope published the "Syllabus of Errors," a denunciation of much of the thought of his age. Included in the condemnation were socialism, communism, rationalism, biblical criticism, and the idea that church and state should be separate. With one enormous push, Pius attempted to topple the entire structure of ideas, building since the Enlightenment, known as modernism. Politically, he opposed

During the last years of papal control over Rome, French troops acted as protectors of the papacy. Facing page, above left, the French defeating Garibaldi's army at Mentana in 1867. Facing page, below left, the First Vatican Council, opened by Pius IX in December 1869. In September 1870, Italian troops breached Porta Pia (below) in Rome; from then on the popes were confined within the walls of the Vatican (right). Center right, Porta Pia. Below right, the coat of arms of Pius IX.

the unification of Italy, which would have meant the surrender of Rome, with all the means at his disposal. The "Syllabus" isolated the pope even further from modernity, and his political ambitions rested on his dependence on France and so visibly increased his vulnerability.

Then in 1869–1870, with French troops surrounding Rome and the cannons of the Italians audible in St. Peter's, Pius climaxed his pontificate and concluded the development of Tridentine Catholicism by having the papacy declared infallible in matters of faith and morals by the First Vatican Council. Many cardinals were still in Rome when the French withdrew and the Italians, on September 20, 1870, entered Rome. Pius retreated into the Vatican and, styling himself "prisoner," waited for the military support which would be generated by international outrage over his captivity. Outrage there was, but the armies never arrived. The pope died in this self-imposed exile in 1878. The Roman people were so resentful of Pius' opposition to Italian unity that they tried to throw his coffin into the Tiber.

The occupation of Rome culminated the long struggle for unification that had been underway in Italy since 1814. At first there was hope, inspired by Italian romantics, that the papacy itself could be the summit and unifying element of the new Italy. Rome's intransigence, however, and the liberal political commitments of the Italian politicians rendered this an impossible fantasy. Most frustrating of all was the papal refusal to give up Rome, the only city which could be the capital of the new Italy.

In 1871, the recently installed Italian government reorganized its relations with the pope. By the "Law of Guarantees," the papacy was deprived of all sovereign rights, and church councils could be held only with the approval of the government. By this one act, the papacy was divested of all political authority and many ecclesiastic privileges.

Throughout the nineteenth century, despite the

With the popes confined to the Vatican, Castel Gandolfo (above left), the papal summer residence outside Rome was turned into a convent. Left, pilgrims thronging St. Peter's, with pious worshipers prostrating themselves before the statue of Saint Peter. Facing page, four of the popes who brought the papacy into the modern era: Leo XIII (above left), the saintly Pius X (above right), Benedict XV (below left), and Pius XI (below right). The first three never set foot outside the Vatican after becoming pope; the fourth finally recognized the Kingdom of Italy.

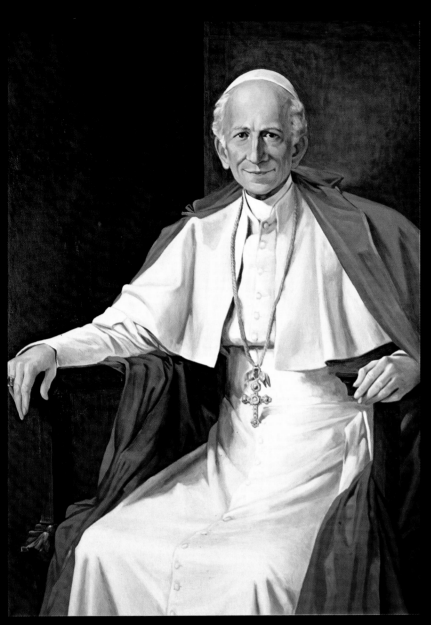

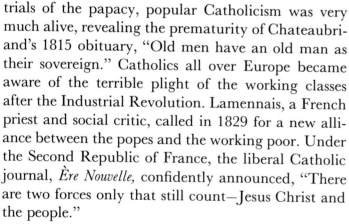

trials of the papacy, popular Catholicism was very much alive, revealing the prematurity of Chateaubriand's 1815 obituary, "Old men have an old man as their sovereign." Catholics all over Europe became aware of the terrible plight of the working classes after the Industrial Revolution. Lamennais, a French priest and social critic, called in 1829 for a new alliance between the popes and the working poor. Under the Second Republic of France, the liberal Catholic journal, *Ère Nouvelle,* confidently announced, "There are two forces only that still count—Jesus Christ and the people."

The papacy discovered this popular church only by slow degrees. In 1891, Leo XIII (1878–1903), who continued to seek restoration of the Papal States, published his encyclical on labor and the working class, the *Rerum Novarum.* Though deeply opposed to any mention of a class struggle and hostile to socialism, Leo called for justice to the working poor and proclaimed their right to a just wage. He inspired Catholic groups to work for social and economic improvement, a varied response which was embraced by the designation "Catholic Action."

The papacy was finally able to gain back some of its temporal sovereignty by the terms of the Lateran

The liberty and independence of the City of the Vatican were established on February 11, 1929, when the papacy and the Italian government signed a treaty formally recognizing the transfer of Rome to Italy. Left, the treaty being signed for the Italian government by Benito Mussolini (above) and for the Vatican by a papal representative, Cardinal Gasparri (below). Since that time five popes have been elected to the papal throne by cardinals meeting behind a locked door (immediately above), and a new Church council, Vatican II, has been held. For many major meetings, cardinals gather in the Sistine Chapel (right).

Agreement of 1929. Mussolini, who was as harsh to his Catholic opponents as he was to the Italian left, wanted to accomplish the grand historical gesture of reconciling church and state, thereby winning papal approval, however tacit, of his regime. Pius XI (1922–1939) signed the agreement by which the papacy accepted the loss of the Papal States in return for a large sum of money and was given temporal authority over the Vatican City. The pope once again became a political ruler, though the new Papal State

was only a symbolic political territory. Paul VI passed a quiet judgment on this agreement when he observed, in 1962, that the loss of the temporal power was one of the "greatest blessings ever received from Christ."

The signing of the Lateran Agreement was an interlude in the development of the contemporary papacy. After the Second World War, the papacy returned to the vision which had begun to take shape under Leo. The identity of this modern papacy was expressed during the second Vatican Council, convened by John XXIII (1958–1963). The council announced the new mission of the Church in language that recalls the medieval hope of cultural unity: "By virtue of her mission to shed on the whole world the radiance of the gospel message, and to unify under one Spirit all men of whatever nation, race, or culture, the Church stands forth as a sign of that brotherliness which allows honest dialogue and invigorates it." The new imperium would be spiritual.

Photography Credits

Lucio Alfieri: p. 10 top right, p. 11, p. 27 bottom left, p. 31 top right/*Arborio-Mella:* p. 96, p. 110 left, p. 111 left, p. 114 bottom right, p. 116 bottom left, p. 131 bottom right/*Bavaria:* p. 130 bottom right and top right/*Bencini:* p. 56, p. 57/*Carrieri:* p. 52 right, p. 62, p. 63, p. 80 top/*Costa:* p. 99 top, p. 106 top and bottom left, p. 107 top right and bottom, p. 110 bottom right, p. 115 bottom right, p. 117 top left, p. 133 bottom, p. 134 bottom, p. 140 top left, p. 145 bottom, p. 150 bottom left and right, p. 151 bottom right, p. 155, p. 156 left, p. 157 top, center, and bottom, p. 160 top, p. 161 bottom, p. 162/*Fiore:* p. 58, p. 64 left, p. 80 center/ *Fioroni:* p. 25 right/*W. Forman:* p. 10 top left and bottom, p. 15 center left, p. 33 bottom right, p. 38 bottom left, p. 40 left and top right, p. 42 center and bottom, p. 46 top, p. 52 left, p. 53/*Giraudon:* p. 114 top/*Lessing:* p. 131 bottom left/*Magnum-Burri:* p. 45 bottom/*Magnum-Capo:* p. 64 right/*Magnum-Hopker:* p. 65 top/*Magnum-Lessing:* p. 55 bottom/*Mairani:* p. 59 top right/*MAS:* p. 29, p. 33 top left, p. 46 bottom, p. 49 top right, p. 50, p. 51 top right and bottom, p. 55 top, p. 66 bottom, p. 67, p. 69 left, p. 76 top, p. 78, p. 82, p. 83, p. 86/*J.P. Paireault:* p. 79 top, pp. 84–85 / *Pellegrini:* p. 14 top left, center first two pictures from left, and bottom right, p. 15 top center, right, center last two pictures from right, and bottom center, p. 17 top, p. 25 left, p. 30 left, p. 68, p. 71, p. 73 bottom right, p. 74 bottom right, p. 77 top and center/*Publiaerfoto:* p. 98 top, p. 122 bottom left/*Publifoto:* p. 23 bottom right, p. 41 right, p. 43 top/*Pucciarelli:* p. 14 bottom center, p. 15 bottom left, p. 42 top, p. 49 top left, p. 70 bottom, p. 77 bottom, p. 91 right, p. 92 bottom left, p. 93, pp. 94–95, p. 97 top, p. 98 bottom left and right, p. 102 top and bottom, p. 103, p. 108 center left, p. 112 bottom left and right, pp. 120–121, p. 122 top, p. 124 top right, bottom left, and right, p. 125 bottom left and right, p. 126 left top and bottom, p. 128 top, p. 129, p. 132 top right and left, p. 135 top right, center, and bottom left, p. 136 top, p. 137 bottom, p. 138 bottom, p. 139, p. 141, p. 142 top left and right, p. 145 top, p. 146, p. 147, p. 149 bottom left, p. 151 top and bottom left, p. 152 top left, p. 154 top left and bottom, p. 158, p. 159 top and bottom left, p. 160 center, p. 161 top left, p. 163 top, p. 165/*Ricatto:* p. 24 center and bottom, p. 26 top, p. 31 left top and bottom, p. 69 top right, p. 79 bottom left/*Ricciarini-Arch. B:* p. 21 bottom, p. 26 bottom, p. 32 left top and bottom, p. 33 top right and bottom left, p. 35 bottom, p. 41 left/*Ricciarini-Cirani:* p. 12, p. 13, p. 38 top right, p. 44 top, p. 80 bottom/*Ricciarini-Moretti:* p. 117 top right, p. 122 bottom right, p. 134 center, p. 138 top, p. 142 bottom left, p. 143 top right, p. 148 bottom, p. 150 top, p. 153 top, p. 156 right/*Ricciarini-P2:* p. 14 center right, p. 15 bottom right, p. 22 left, p. 28, p. 31 bottom right, p. 35 center, p. 45 top, p. 59 top left and bottom left/*Ricciarini-Simion:* p. 108 right, p. 127, p. 159 bottom right, p. 163 bottom left, p. 166 top left/ *Ricciarini-Tomsich:* p. 14 top center and bottom left, p. 15 top left, p. 20 top left, p. 23 top right, p. 35 top, p. 90 right, p. 133 top, p. 140 top right, bottom left, and right, p. 144 top, p. 148 top, p. 164 bottom/*Archivio Rizzoli:* p. 24 top, p. 38 top left, p. 89, p. 99 bottom right, p. 110 top right, p. 111 right, p. 113, p. 114 bottom left, p. 115 top and bottom left, p. 116 bottom right, p. 118, p. 119 bottom, p. 124 top left, p. 130 top left, p. 136 bottom, p. 137 top, p. 149 top, p. 152 center, p. 153 bottom, p. 163 bottom right, p. 166 top right, p. 167/*Scala:* p. 32 right, p. 43 bottom, p. 51 top left, pp. 104–105, p. 112 top left, p. 116 top left and right, p. 119 top, p. 128 bottom, p. 135 bottom right/*S.E.F.:* p. 18, p. 19, p. 23 left, p. 38 bottom right, p. 59 bottom right, p. 74 top, p. 76 bottom, p. 90 left, p. 97 bottom, p. 108 top left, p. 125 top right, p. 149 bottom right, p. 154 top right, p. 160 bottom, p. 161 top and right, p. 163 center right/*Sheridan:* pp. 60–61/*Sheridan-Stirling:* p. 16/*Spielmann:* p. 130 top right/*Titus:* p. 9, p. 14 top right, p. 20 bottom left and top right, p. 21 top, p. 22 right, p. 27 top and bottom right, p. 30 right, p. 34, p. 39 top right, p. 40 bottom, p. 44 bottom, p. 46 top, p. 47, p. 48, p. 54, p. 66 top, p. 70 center right, p. 75, p. 81, p. 87 left, center right, and bottom right, p. 91 top left, p. 92 top left, p. 99 bottom left, p. 106 top right, p. 109, p. 112 top right, p. 123 top left, right, and bottom, p. 131 top right and center, p. 134 top, p. 135 top left, p. 143 top left, p. 161 center right, p. 164 top/*A. Zecca:* p. 65 bottom, p. 69 bottom, p. 70 top left, right, and center left, p. 72, p. 74 center and bottom left, p. 79 bottom right, p. 87 top right.

Index